P9-CJY-027

JOURNALISM

Ian Hargreaves

JOURNALISM

TRUTH OR DARE?

OXFORD
UNIVERSITY PRESS

OXFORD
UNIVERSITY PRESS

Great Clarendon Street, Oxford OX2 6DP

Oxford University Press is a department of the University of Oxford.
It furthers the University's objective of excellence in research, scholarship,
and education by publishing worldwide in

Oxford New York

Auckland Bangkok Buenos Aires Cape Town Chennai
Dar es Salaam Delhi Hong Kong Istanbul Karachi Kolkata
Kuala Lumpur Madrid Melbourne Mexico City Mumbai Nairobi
São Paulo Shanghai Taipei Tokyo Toronto

Oxford is a registered trade mark of Oxford University Press
in the UK and in certain other countries

Published in the United States
by Oxford University Press Inc., New York

First published 2003

British Library Cataloguing in Publication Data
Data available

Library of Congress Cataloging in Publication Data
Data available

ISBN 0-19-280274-7

Typeset in Minion and Formatta
by RefineCatch Limited, Bungay, Suffolk
Printed in Great Britain by
TJ International Ltd, Padstow, Cornwall

To Ben, Kelda, Yoko, Zola, and Adele

Acknowledgements

Countless people have contributed without knowing it to the thinking in this book, especially my fellow-journalists at the *Keighley News*, the *Bradford Telegraph and Argus*, the *Financial Times*, the BBC, the *Independent*, and the *New Statesman*, my main places of work in the last thirty years.

I would not have got to the arduous task of book-writing had I not, in 1998, taken up a position at the Centre for Journalism Studies at Cardiff University. There, Professor John Hartley encouraged me to think that the ruminations of experience might be turned into something more worthwhile than anecdotage. I was surprised and impressed by the passion he brought to his arguments about journalism. Professional journalists, especially British ones, are given to disdain for the work of media scholars like Hartley; but my time in Cardiff convinced me that journalists would do a better job if they encouraged interrogation of the way they work and paused to listen, converse, and think. I shall always live in awe of someone able to include in his own publications list a piece with the title: *Why is it Scholarship when Someone Wants to Kill you? Truth as Violence.*

I am also in very specific debt to a number of friends, most of them journalists, who involved themselves directly or indirectly in the discussions that have taken place around this book. Some were even generous enough to read and comment upon early drafts. I would especially like to thank Richard Ayre, Tom Bentley, John Lloyd, Stewart Fleming, Tony Hall, and Chris Cramer.

At Oxford University Press, Katharine Reeve had the idea of commissioning the book and helped shape its content. Rebecca O'Connor has been a patient tolerator of broken deadlines.

Roch, Pembrokeshire
January 2003

Contents

List of illustrations

Introduction

The Paradox of Power

Journalism entered the twenty-first century caught in a paradox of its own making. We have more news and more influential journalism, across an unprecedented range of media, than at any time since the birth of the free press in the eighteenth century; yet journalism is also under widespread attack, from politicians, philosophers, the general public, and even from journalists themselves. This book is an attempt to explain this paradox through a new position, from which journalists can defend their work and their privileges, based upon a clearer understanding of the place they now occupy in public life.

The ascent in journalism's influence is easily explained. Its underlying cause is the growth in the cultural, political, and economic value of information, facilitated by the emergence of new, cheap electronic technologies to distribute and display news. It is now widely understood that, without abundant and accessible information, we can have neither the democracy in which we believe nor the economic growth and consumer choice we desire.

News, which was once difficult and expensive to obtain, today surrounds us like the air we breathe. Much of it is literally ambient: displayed on computers, public billboards, trains, aircraft, and mobile phones. Where once news had to be sought out in expensive and scarce news sheets, today it is ubiquitous and very largely free at the point of consumption. Satisfying news hunger no longer involves a twice daily diet of a morning newspaper and evening TV news bulletin: news comes in snack-form, to be grazed, and at every level of quality. Where once journalism's reach was confined by the time it took to haul bundles of newsprint from one end of a country to the other, now it is global, instantaneous, and interactive.

But there are problems with this new culture of news. Because there is so much of it, we find it difficult to sort the good from the bad. The fact that it is mostly obtainable without direct payment means that we value it less. As a generation grows up unaccustomed to the idea that news costs money, the economics of certain types of resource-intensive journalism are undermined.

Also, when information travels as fast as it does today, it can wreak destruction before there is time for it to be understood or even considered. In the world of instant journalism, reputations are destroyed and privacies trivially invaded in the time it takes to switch TV channels. Junk food may be convenient and taste OK at the first bite, but its popularity raises questions of public health. So too with news. Today's television journalists shoot pictures in desert war-zones and beam them via satellite for transmission around the world. These stories get most prominence if the shots are visually exciting: violence is desirable, death a bonus. Better still if the journalist is young, glamorous, and famous. Less melodramatic, but more important stories, about education, health, and community relations, get less coverage. Meanwhile financial journalists are hard-wired to market information systems and deliver instant appraisal which moves prices, tempting journalists to profit personally from their insider knowledge. The circumstances of modern news thus test the journalist's judgement and honesty, not in fundamentally new ways, but more routinely and at greater speed than ever before. If the journalist is secretly playing the market, or the tool of some invisible public relations machine, the public interest is betrayed.

In politics, democracy itself is at stake in this world of high-speed, always-on news. Political reporters pronounce sudden verdicts upon the politicians they often outshine in fame and, as a result, parliaments everywhere feel themselves reduced to side-attractions in the great non-stop media show. In 1828, the British historian Macaulay dubbed the press gallery in Parliament a 'fourth estate' of the realm.[1] Today, the news media appear to many to have become the first estate, able to topple monarchs and turn Parliament into a talking shop which ceases to exist if journalists turn their backs. Television interviewers wag their fingers and arch their eyebrows at government ministers, called to account in the headmaster's studio, live, before a mass audience. Since more people vote in reality television shows than in elections for the European Parliament or municipal authorities, the response of politicians has been to try, desperately, to be more like television: conversational, friendly, emotional, and not too demanding. How else can Congressmen and parliamentarians retain the interest of the young? How else to be heard through the cacophony of information overload?

Journalism in Trouble

There are many symptoms of the difficulties now mounting up around this pervasive journalism. We know, from opinion surveys, that journalists are less trusted and less esteemed than used to be the case. Surveys rank journalists low in public affection, alongside the politicians they have helped drag down, but behind business executives and civil servants and way behind the most respected professionals such as doctors, teachers, and scientists.[2] 'The future for the press in the new millennium looks bleak,' says Dr Carl Jensen, founder of Project Censored, which has been tracking press issues in the US for twenty-five years.

The press has the power to stimulate people to clean up the environment, prevent nuclear proliferation, force crooked politicians out of office, reduce poverty, provide quality health care for all people and even to save the lives of millions of people as it did in Ethiopia in 1984. But instead, we are using it to promote sex, violence, and sensationalism and to line the pockets of already wealthy media moguls.[3]

Jensen's view was widely echoed in the United States during the scandal that engulfed President Bill Clinton in the late 1990s over his sexual misbehaviour with the White House intern Monica Lewinsky. The American news media, including some of its most highly reputed newspapers and broadcasters, were widely acknowledged to be peddling gossip, rumour, and unchecked facts as they scrambled to outdo each other for sensation and scoops. Critics saw this as part of a pattern, evident in coverage of an earlier celebrity scandal, the O. J. Simpson trial, when the news media were accused of caring too much about soap opera and too little about justice. The public's reaction to President Clinton's 'Zippergate' was to turn against the news media, rather than the president. The fact that journalists all over the world so casually add the suffix 'gate' to any story, however trivial, which involves political scandal underlines a certain loss of seriousness since the days of Watergate and the Pentagon Papers.

Concerned Journalists Fight Back

Through events like these, scepticism about journalism has started to eat at the soul of American democratic values. According to a 1999 poll, 53 per cent of Americans, reared on the First Amendment, that forbids any curtailment of the right to free expression of individuals or newspapers, had reached the conclusion that the press has too much freedom.[4] At the same time, a movement of 'concerned journalists' has emerged, advocating a return to basic professional standards of accurate and balanced reporting and campaigning against what it sees as increasingly concentrated, commercial ownership of news media. The new owners, say the concerned journalists, are deflecting journalism from its sacred mission to inform citizens without fear and favour, pandering instead to the appetites of shareholders for quarter-on-quarter profits growth. 'We are facing the possibility that independent news will be replaced by self-interested commercialism posing as news,' say the authors of one of the movement's manifestos.

> The First Amendment—that a free press is an independent institution—is threatened for the first time in our history without government meddling. In this world, the First Amendment becomes a property right establishing ground rules for free economic competition, not free speech. This is a fundamental and epic change with enormous implications for democratic society.[5]

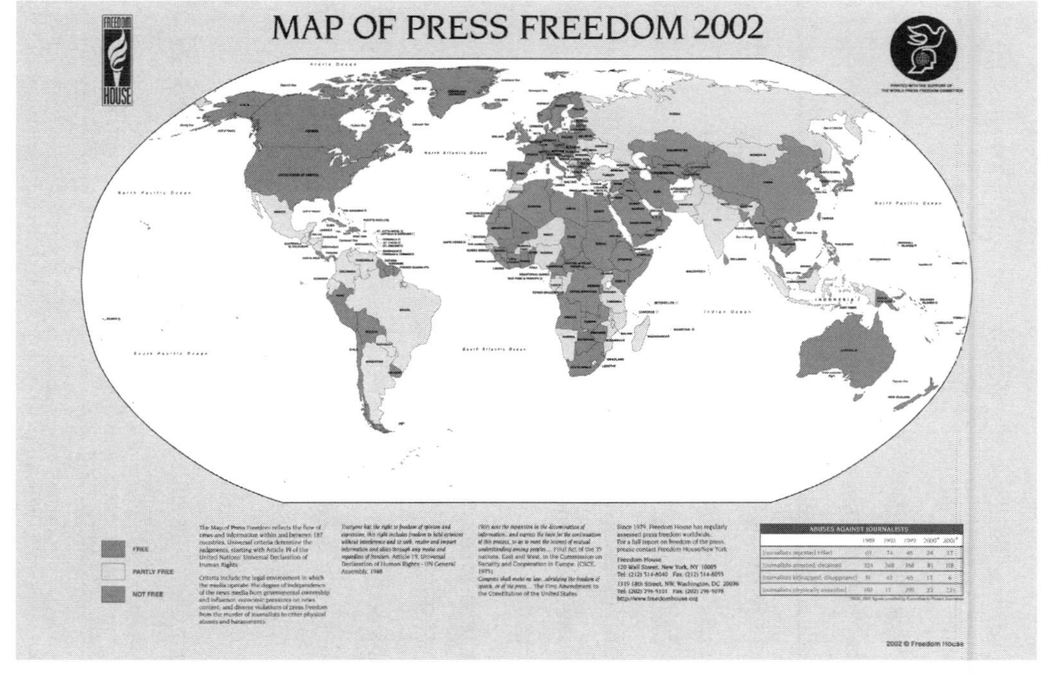

1. World Press Freedom Map. The modern struggle for press freedom is roughly 350 years old, but still campaigning organizations regard huge tracts of the world as lacking free news media.

A similar story can be heard, in one form or another, all over the democratic world, though it is more intense in some places than others. In Italy, the Prime Minister, Silvio Berlusconi, is regarded by his critics as commanding patronage in the state broadcasting system, RAI, as well as still benefiting from his history as a dominant figure in a private company, Mediaset, which owns most of Italy's commercial television. In effect, say his critics, Berlusconi pulls the strings in 90 per cent of the country's television journalism which is, as result, fatally compromised. Berlusconi says that today he exercises influence in neither Mediaset nor state broadcasting, but Vaclav Havel, President of the Czech Republic, and veteran of one of Europe's more recent fights for free media, the Velvet Revolution, chose World Press Freedom Day in 2002 to issue a warning. 'In a situation where there will be no direct political oppression and censorship,' he said, 'there might be more complex issues, especially at the economic level, that may affect freedom of speech. Italy might represent an early form of this problem.'[6]

In Britain which, unlike the US, does not have a written constitution, but which has incorporated into domestic law the European Convention of Human Rights and its freedom of expression clause, there has also been a sustained pattern of public concern. Here the agenda focuses upon the powerful position of the Australian–American Rupert Murdoch, who controls over a third of the national newspaper market and owns the country's dominant pay television platform. Murdoch is regarded by many as an outsider capable of making or breaking governments. There is also persistent anxiety about lax standards in the press, which is widely felt to be guilty of insensitivity towards public feeling on issues such as personal privacy. A defining moment in British journalism was the violent death of Princess Diana in a Parisian subway in August 1997, her car chased by freelance photographers employed by British (and other) newspapers. At the Princess's funeral, her brother accused publishers of having 'blood on their hands'. Throughout the 1990s, the Press Complaints Commission, a self-regulatory body that oversees with debatable effectiveness an editor's code of ethics, struggled to update its rules to meet public and political pressure. The PCC's reputation was not helped when, in 2002, its chairman, Lord Wakeham, a former minister in the government of Margaret Thatcher, turned out to be a director of Enron, the American energy company that cooked its books. Wakeham was forced to step down from the PCC, to be replaced by the retiring ambassador to Washington, Sir Christopher Meyer, another establishment figure charged with the task of burnishing the press's troubled image.

A New Challenge to Press Freedom

It was in this atmosphere that Dr Onora O'Neill, the philosopher and principal of Newnham College, Cambridge, delivered the 2002 Reith Lectures, a prestigious series named in honour of the first director general of the BBC. She argued that the classic eighteenth-century doctrine of press freedom had outlived its usefulness; that it belonged to a more heroic time. In modern democracies, press freedom was being used as a cloak to shield media conglomerates' domination of public discussion 'in which misinformation may be peddled uncorrected and in which reputations may be selectively shredded or magnified. A free press is not an unconditional good'.[7] When the media misleads, she added, 'the wells of public discourse and public life are poisoned'.

O'Neill's argument chimes worryingly with American concerns about abuse of the First Amendment. It is a weighty argument, with many more colourful predecessors. Alan Clark, a colourful British Conservative Member of Parliament, in an essay written just before his death, dismissed journalists as: 'fellows with, in the main, squalid and unfulfilling private lives, insecure in their careers, and suffering a considerable degree of dependence on alcohol and narcotics.'[8] This is a judgement less maverick than it sounds. Conrad (Lord) Black, a substantial Canadian publisher with interests in Britain, North America, and Israel, has characterized journalists as 'ignorant, lazy, opinionated, intellectually dishonest, and inadequately supervised'. A more searching version of the moral case against journalistic practice was assembled by Janet Malcolm in her study of a dispute between a convicted murderer and a journalist who wrote an account of the criminal's life. This is how Malcolm, whose other subjects have included the life of the American poet Sylvia Plath, drum-rolls her central argument at the opening of her essay:

Every journalist who is not too stupid or full of himself to notice what is going on knows that what he does is morally indefensible. He is a kind of confidence man, preying upon people's vanity, ignorance or loneliness, gaining their trust and betraying them without remorse ... Journalists justify their treachery in various ways according to their temperaments. The more pompous talk about freedom of speech and 'the public's right to know'; the least talented talk about Art; the seemliest murmur about earning a living.'[9]

Anyone who has worked for a long time in journalism and thought about what they are doing will recognize that there is some force in these characterizations. Journalism stands accused of sacrificing accuracy for speed, purposeful investigation for cheap intrusion and reliability for entertainment. 'Dumbed down' news media are charged with privileging sensation over significance and celebrity over achievement. The plaything of corporate public relations experts and other self-servers, modern journalism is found to be not so much a public service as a public health hazard.

The End of Journalism?

The response of journalists to this charge sheet is not uniform. Many journalists share the anxieties of the 'concerned journalists' of the United States. They can see that greater concentration of corporate ownership of the news media is cutting newsroom budgets and undermining journalistic integrity, giving advertisers and sponsors unwarranted influence over news agendas and even the composition of individual news items. 'Too many once-distinguished news organisations have lost their lustre; too few new ones have materialised,' say two senior *Washington Post* figures.[10] Journalists also worry about the effects of new media technologies, which some think are turning them into 'robohacks' rather than reporters and editors,[11] something that may even prefigure 'the end of journalism'. There is concern about the polarization of the news media with, at one end, badly paid and sometimes inadequately trained young people in smaller newspapers, radio stations, and magazines, and at the other a handful of celebrity journalists who present television shows or write columns for the big newspapers and earn showbusiness salaries.

Paul Foot, a distinguished radical, journalistic investigator, has lamented the death of investigative journalism[12] and John Pilger, the campaigning Australian journalist, who works in television and print, has complained at the ease with which most journalists are duped into following the 'hidden agenda' of political or business power.[13] Other journalists express alarm at the casual, amoral blood-thirstiness of modern journalism towards elected politicians; the trend, in Adam Gopnik's words, from dining with presidents to dining on them. As John Lloyd, a writer for the *Financial Times* and the *New York Times*, has said: the famous dictum of Harold Evans, who edited the London *Sunday Times* in the 1970s, that the journalist interviewing a politician should always ask 'why is this bastard lying to me?' has 'passed from radical fearlessness to a commercial strategy with big implications for the health of our public life'.[14] Lloyd calls for new mechanisms to 'interrogate the interrogators' and it is no coincidence that in recent years, book-shelves have filled with mournful or polemical tomes about the decline of journalism, many of them written by journalists. Their titles or subtitles illustrate their spirit: *American Journalism in Peril; How Showbiz Values are Corrupting the News*; *Newszak and News Media*; the *Sound Bite Society*; and *Down the Tube*, to name but a handful.

Crisis, What Crisis?

There is, however, a second type of response to the attack on the professional standards of journalism, which asks, with a world-weary expression: 'crisis, what crisis?' Journalists and journalism, these people say, have always been under attack and always will be: the more ferocious the attack, the healthier journalism must be. Janet Malcolm's confidence trickster is a necessary agent of society's ability to examine and purge itself; omelettes cannot be made without the breaking of eggs. There is, in this view, no case for agitation about the way that journalists frame their ethical codes, get trained and are regulated.

This insouciance is well captured in a widely quoted piece of advice given to young people desperate for a start in journalism. It came from Nicolas Tomalin, a star reporter for the *Sunday Times*, who was killed in the Yom Kippur War in 1973. Tomalin, having navigated an effortless passage from Cambridge University, via Fleet Street gossip columns to a top job on a leading newspaper, advised aspiring reporters that 'the only qualities essential for real success in journalism are ratlike cunning, a plausible manner and a little literary ability'.[15] Much the same line emerges in the writings of H. L. Mencken, the great Baltimore iconoclast, who thought journalism 'a craft to be mastered in four days and abandoned at the first sign of a better job'. No inflated comparisons here between journalists, doctors, scientists, and lawyers and certainly no acceptance of the case for self-examination. Journalism is strong, precisely because it makes no high-flown claims for itself or its practitioners.

Nestling in the folds of Mencken's irony lies a serious point. Journalism, he says, cannot be likened to professions such as medicine and the law because the journalist 'is unable, as yet, to control admission to his craft'. Indeed, the only societies where admission to the practice of journalism is or has been controlled are those that have abandoned or never known democracy, such as the Soviet Union in the cold war period, or numerous countries in Africa, the Middle East, and Asia today. The requirement to belong to a state-endorsed 'union of journalists' or 'press club' guarantees that real journalism, if it exists at all, will take place by subterfuge. The core democratic right to free expression gives every citizen the right to be a journalist, to report a fact, and to publish an opinion: journalism, by this line of reasoning, is philosophically and practically beyond regulation by any body associated with the state. Even to place too heavy an emphasis upon training or professional standards can diminish this necessary freedom: just as free expression guarantees tolerance for pornography and bad novels, so too, it must avert its eyes from bad journalism. The alternative is to turn journalism into another branch of established power.

Yet there is something too easy and evasive in Mencken and Tomalin for our own times, when the mass media exercise global, corporate power on an unprecedented scale. Journalism today reflects not so much the motivations of clamorous individual citizens as the motivations of vast, often highly profitable institutions. To do its job in a modern society, journalism needs the capital such organizations provide, but with that power comes a new calculus of power against responsibility; unconstrained freedom versus legitimate check by a civil society whose own values may be threatened by the new, global hyper-journalism. Journalists need to remember that it is only through that same civil society or public sphere that they have secured and maintained their privileges: protection against unreasonable constraints from libel law and, increasingly, other branches of commercial law, such as copyright and intellectual property. The point is that in return, the public has a right to expect that journalists will take seriously the responsibilities that come with their privileges. Journalists are not lone rangers with a pocket full of silver bullets; they are individuals operating within an understood economic, cultural, and political framework. That is why journalists should welcome the new mood of interrogation about their values, standards, and professional practices. In the pages which follow I have to develop that interrogation.

New Technology, New Politics

There is another, important sense in which the framework of discussion assumed by a Mencken or a Tomalin is anachronistic. Both writers are making an argument that is, essentially, confined to newspaper journalism, at a time when newspapers are, in all advanced societies, in decline. American research reports that, today, a minority of people say that they read a newspaper the previous day, compared with 58 per cent only a decade ago.[16] In Britain, more than a quarter of people today do not regard newspapers as an important source of news, whereas almost everyone makes some use of television news.[17] This change is of huge significance, not least because of the difference in political and economic culture which attended the birth of the press and the electronic media. Newspapers have their roots in commercial markets and a period when citizens were struggling, via their newspapers, for democratic rights. By contrast, radio was born on the threshold of a totalitarian era in Europe and, for technical reasons, developed initially either as a state monopoly or an oligopoly licensed by the state, based upon the state's ownership of broadcast spectrum. Television, which came to maturity in the second half of the century, also involved very strong state influence, either through licensing, in democracies, or direct control in more authoritarian settings. As General de Gaulle, the French president, once remarked: 'My enemies have the press, so I keep television.'[18] De Gaulle's successors have, like their peers in other European countries, presided over a significant loosening of monopoly, but no one doubts the influence the French government still exerts in television, through its appointments to the country's regulatory system and other less obvious means. Television, in most parts of the world, remains a heavily regulated industry, especially with regard to its news services.

In the third era of electronic news media, based around the internet and other broadband communications technologies, the formative creative and political cultures are different again, this time involving a fusion of economic liberalism and globalization with a technology rooted partly in the Pentagon and partly in the world's leading research universities. It is hard to say whether the political culture of the internet has been more influenced by American West Coast libertarianism, communitarianism, European social democracy, or the ideas of contemporary business. What we can say is that the internet creates a space for convergence between broadcasters and newspapers, which now compete with each other directly on the World Wide Web. It is an open question where this leaves the state and its regulators. The technology seems to point in the direction of greater freedom, since the internet bursts wide open national jurisdictions of content regulation, but the evidence of contemporary debate and public opinion is that we may not be happy to see journalism left entirely to its own devices. We fear, in Onora O'Neill's words, that market forces alone may not prevent the poisoning of the wells of public discourse.

The effects of these waves of technological change upon the culture, ethics, and practice of journalism have already been profound. British law, for example, still today requires that all television and radio news services be politically impartial and accurate—and regulators have powers to intervene where this is not the case. Meanwhile, the largest media organization in the UK by a considerable margin is not Rupert Murdoch's diverse interests but the BBC, a publicly owned body which controls half the radio market, 40 per cent of television, and has been among the largest, if not *the* largest, investor in on-line content in Europe. Some see these arrangements as a persistent mechanism for political, or perhaps more accurately establishment control of the most powerful news medium, but it is perhaps more accurately seen as a deliberate, Gaullist denial of influence to the market forces that shaped the press. Since research suggests that the British public trusts the news it gets from television much more than it trusts what it reads in newspapers, even though British newspaper consumption is also very high by international standards, politicians are justified in claiming that there is public support for these arrangements.[19] In the United

States, by contrast, the most serious alarm about the decline in journalistic quality relates to television, and especially to the decline in the news divisions of the television networks. Is it possible that Americans will lose faith in the deregulatory course followed by all administrations since President Reagan's? If not, how will American journalism develop a response to its critics? Will the market be judged capable of delivering satisfactory solutions?

What cannot be denied is that the new digital technologies have started to cause radical shifts in the ways in which everyone consumes news. That is true of the elderly Afro-Caribbean ladies I watched sitting in the public library in Peckham, South London, on a rainy Saturday afternoon reading the *Jamaica Gleaner* newspaper, on-line. It is also true of Arab communities around the world, which can today access via satellite and cable television systems a global Arabic-language television news service, Al Jazeera, which has become well known since the terrorist attacks on New York and Washington in September 2001 and which offers a serious challenge to the hegemony of global news services owned by Americans or former colonial powers like Britain and France. Many ethnic and linguistic diasporas are finding that they can defend their cultural identities, or even acquire muscular new ones, as a direct result of enhanced media connectivity. Take the example of Wales, a tiny country on the very edge of Europe with a population of 3 million people, of whom approximately one-fifth speak Welsh, one of Europe's oldest languages. Today, as a result of investment by BBC Wales in an on-line news service, that community has for the first time a written daily news service, in effect an electronic daily newspaper, in the Welsh language. This is, naturally, very welcome to Welsh speakers, but it is not something that could possibly have been delivered, in present conditions, on a commercial basis.

Meanwhile, fast-moving young entrepreneurs are grabbing their latest news alerts on telephones and 'personal digital assistants' and other electronic news services cater for specialized interest groups, ranging from cancer sufferers to anti-capitalist campaigners, the latter styling their own 'anti-media' organizations 'independent media centres'. 'Anyone with a modem can report to the world,' says Matt Drudge, the Hollywood-based internet journalist and gossip-monger, whose work precipitated crisis at the Clinton White House.

New News, New Democracy

According to some commentators, this burgeoning supply of new services tells us that journalism, far from dumbing down to a new irrelevance, is diversifying to an unprecedented health and influence. John Hartley, a British academic who works in Australia, calls journalism 'the sense-making practice of modernity', the very foundation of democratic politics and the primary wiring of popular culture.[20] Hartley and others like him, view the so-called 'tabloidization' of journalism not as a diminution of its ambition, but as an extension of its reach, another unfolding layer in the story of journalism's role as the oxygen of democracy.

These proponents of what is sometimes called the 'the new news' say that the 'concerned journalists' of the Ivy League American newspaper industry are simply failing to get the point that they are in the process of being swept aside by a less rule-based type of journalism, that works via email, text-messaging, multimedia story-telling, web-logging, consumer magazines, popular music, and a host of other media yet to be invented. Rap music, it has been said, is 'the CNN black people never had'. The 'old news,' say the new news radicals, is like the old politics, simply not of any interest to younger people, and the old-timers should get on a new road if they can't lend a hand. There are certainly figures to support this depiction of a *nouvelle vague* in news. By 2000, more than one in three Americans, and half of Americans under the age of 30, were going on-line at least once a week to pick up news.[21] British research in 2002 found that the internet was regarded as the main source of news by a significant group of young British Asians, who do not consider themselves well served by mainstream news media.[22] This same research, however, also found that the type of news gathered on-line was more global than local, and more concerned with sport and entertainment than with politics.

In the US, regular viewing of network television news fell from 38 per cent to 30 per cent of the population in the two short years between 1998 and 2000, as it was squeezed not only by the internet but also by cable news services. Newspaper consumption is falling very sharply among young people. In a recent survey, only 30 per cent of Americans in their thirties said they had read a newspaper the previous day, down from a figure of 53 per cent a decade earlier. This does not mean, however, that young people are not reading. The same survey showed that Americans under the age of 50 read lots of magazines and are as likely to have read a book as a newspaper the previous day. 'Young people are reading everything but newspapers,' says Andrew Kohut, director of the Pew Research Centre for the People and the Press.[23] In Britain, the same edition of *Prospect Magazine* which contained John Lloyd's newspaperman's lament for journalism's decline, carried an article about book publishing which proclaimed 'a new golden age of the printed word'.[24] To speak of the headlong decline of 'the media' or 'the news media' is to indulge in crass over-simplification.

Think Before you Kick

This book involves an attempt to describe and analyse the forces at work upon contemporary journalism and to judge the concerns of the defenders of 'old news' values against the enthusiasms of the 'new news' generation. I operate from the assumption that journalism matters not just to journalists, but to everyone: good journalism provides the information and opinion upon which successful democratic societies depend. Corrupt that and you corrupt everything. But, equally, let journalism ossify, or be economically undermined, and politics and public life will suffer.

The discussion that follows entails some historical background, about the emergence of the idea of a free press, the rise of newspapers, radio, television and new media, and the growth of public relations, which was intimately connected with the development of both journalism and democratic politics in the last century. But this is not a history book. It is the reflection of a journalist who happens, in the last thirty years, to have enjoyed a rather unusual career, working all over the world, and in all media.

I started as a local newspaper reporter in northern England and spent a decade reporting for the *Financial Times*, one of the world's few global newspapers. I then ran the BBC's vast news and current affairs operation during a period of its reinvigoration in the late 1980s before becoming in succession: deputy editor of the *Financial Times* and editor of the *Independent*, a position from which I was fired at the end of 1995. That took me to the editor's chair of the *New Statesman*, a great political weekly, founded by Fabian Socialists nearly a hundred years ago, before taking time out for reflection in Britain's oldest journalism school at Cardiff, where I continued to make radio and televison documentaries and write for newspapers on a freelance basis.

These diverse experiences have given me the privilege of working alongside some of the world's best journalists, for some of the world's best news media organizations. But I have also worked for a boss accused of serious dishonesty and I have encountered the worst kind of news room bullies, the sort of people who regard inquiring foreign journalism as inexplicable concern for 'dead black babies'. Most recently, I have taken on a role inside a major UK business, where I will no doubt add to my understanding of the way that journalism works, along with a parallel role on the board of Britain's new regulatory body for the communications and media sectors: Ofcom.

One reporter who rang to ask me about my new role in corporate communications, for BAA, which runs most of Britain's airports, took no trouble to conceal her contempt that a journalist could have agreed to work for a large business. 'The job of journalists is to give everyone a good kicking,' she said. In my view, the job of journalists is to work out what's going on before they put the boot in. Too few can be bothered with this, the harder part of good journalism.

One thing I have learnt as a journalist is that all journalism is defined, to some extent, by the institutions within which it is created, and that every type of institution brings strengths and weakness to the mission of journalism. BBC journalism is magnificent in its range, carefulness, and resources, but it does tend towards an establishment view of the world. That is probably inevitable, given its funding structure and governance. Journalism on the *New Statesman*, by contrast, where our annual editorial budget would not have covered the taxi bills of a tiny division of the BBC, was about finding new ideas and new angles, missed by the mainstream press, in pursuit of a politically committed view of the world. What is obvious to anyone who has worked in journalism is that we need many and competing cultures of ownership if our news media are to be truly diverse and, consequently, trusted. Non-diverse journalism cannot, by definition, achieve trust across the whole range of a public which is itself so diverse in terms of economic circumstance, class, ethnicity, gender, region, and in many other ways. Nor can a journalism which lacks diversity and plurality adapt to ceaseless change. If journalism cannot be both trusted and adaptable, it has no value.

It will by now be obvious that I did not set out to write this book entirely convinced by the arguments of the 'old news' people, the 'concerned journalists' of the United States. Whilst I have been raised with and share their commitment to old-fashioned virtues like accuracy and truth-telling in journalism, I suspect that there is in their response to the 'new news' something of the *ancien régime*, alarmed at the cry of the mob in the street. Matt Drudge, the bloggers, 24-hour TV news channels, 'investigative comedy' and even celebrity journalists and creative public relations are all part of the wave of energy and innovation which journalism and public communications constantly needs to refresh itself: they may be part of journalism's necessary diversity, and self-interrogation, rather than its enemy.

Where we are all agreed is that fresh, trenchant, bracing journalism is the oxygen not only of democracy but of cultural exchange. The contest between the state, its citizens, and journalism, and the remaking of the terms of the relationship between them, is a relentlessly moving diorama. As John Keane, one of our best writers on democracy, has said: 'freedom of communications is an ongoing project without an ultimate solution. It is a project which constantly generates new constellations and dilemmas and contradictions.'[25]

But the underlying mission of journalism itself does not change. It is to provide the information and argument that enables societies to work through their disagreements and to know their priorities. And it is a job done well only when accomplished with style and impact: when the words flow and the pictures are immaculately sequenced. Unlike poetry, which as W. H. Auden said, 'makes nothing happen' and 'survives in the valley of its making where executives would never want to tamper',[26] journalism only exists when it strides out into the world and demands a response. Executives and politicians will always want to tamper with the work of journalists.

1

Born Free

Press Freedom and Beyond

Journalism is not an easy business. In the year 2001 alone, thirty-seven journalists were known to have been killed in the course of doing their jobs. It was the highest figure since 1994, when seventy-two journalists died.

Such deaths mostly go unnoticed. An exception was the case of Daniel Pearl, the *Wall Street Journal* reporter, who was murdered in such grim circumstances that it constituted a 'story'. Pearl, 38, had set out to understand the workings of militant Islamic networks in Europe following the suicide attacks on New York and Washington in September 2001. His inquiries took him to Pakistan, where he was kidnapped and held in captivity before having his throat slit, while his murderers recorded their actions. The resulting videotape, showing a man brandishing a severed head, was then handed to American officials, to ensure that the murder made its maximum impact. Pearl's pregnant wife said her husband had always felt impelled to go where the story led. Of the other thirty-six journalists killed that year, eight died in the space of a few weeks as American troops opened up the battle to take control of Afghanistan from the Taliban. There were more Western casualties among the media in this war than in the American-led alliance directing it.

But it does not require a war for journalists to die. According to the Committee to Protect Journalists, most of the thirty-seven killed in 2001 'were murdered in reprisal for their reporting on sensitive topics, including official crime and corruption in countries such as Bangladesh, China, Thailand and Yugoslavia'. During 2001, the CPJ recorded 118 cases of journalists being jailed, mostly from 'little noticed crackdowns in Eritrea and Nepal, carried out after September 11,' which provided an excuse for despots all over the world to brand their political opponents as 'terrorists' unworthy of basic human rights. In Zimbabwe, President Robert Mugabe used precisely this formulation in order to expel numerous journalists ahead of a general election. China, in 2001, maintained its long reputation as the world's leading jailer of journalists, ending the year with thirty-five journalists behind bars. All told, the CPJ reported 500 cases of media repression in 140 countries. Not that we should think these incidents occur only in faraway places with primitive political cultures. In recent years, a number of journalists have been killed in Ireland. One, Veronica Guerin, was shot in her car by gangsters in Dublin in June 1996. A year earlier, a masked man had entered her home, pointed a gun at her head and then shot her in the thigh. She carried on her investigations, with the comment: 'I am letting the public know exactly how this society operates.'

The bleak chronicles maintained by organizations like CPJ and Index on Censorship provide a necessary reminder that the battle for the most basic news media freedom is still being fought against heavy odds in many places. Authoritarian governments have proved almost as adept at circumscribing use of new communications technologies like the internet, as they have always been at suppressing undesired elements in the press and broadcasting. China, for example, routes all internet traffic through officially controlled pipelines, blocking any material it wishes to deny its citizens, and has engaged in running battles with several Western media organizations, including the internet search company Google.

Index on Censorship, however, is clear that state encroachment upon news media freedom is by no means confined to undemocratic regimes in the less developed parts of the world. Following the Al Qaeda attacks on the United States, Index criticized the almost uniformly subservient tone of American news media towards the Bush administration's threatened curtailments of civil liberties, which included at one point an explicit proposal to set up a division within the Pentagon to furnish misleading information to the news media. There was no doubt, however, that the Bush administration enjoyed strong popular support for measures to hold the news media in line and that the American public largely expected their news media to cooperate with the authorities.[1] Index also reported that the US State Department had demanded that Sheikh Hamid bin Khalifa al-Thani, the emir of Qatar in the Arabian Gulf, apply pressure to the respected Arab-language television station Al Jazeera, based in Qatar, to make its reports more sympathetic to American interests. Al Jazeera had acquired notoriety as the vehicle through which videotapes made by Osama bin Laden, the leader of the group that attacked New York and Washington, reached television audiences worldwide. According to Index's filing, the emir resisted American pressures, pointing out that Al Jazeera had won a huge following throughout the Arab world precisely because of its editorial independence. It was one of many ironies of the war on terrorism that the unelected head of a small country lacking the most basic mechanisms of democracy should find himself lecturing the leader of the world's most powerful democracy. Index added tersely: 'The United States eventually resolved the issue by destroying the station's Kabul office with an air strike on November 13, 2001.'[2] This was something of an exaggeration, since Al Jazeera's tiny Kabul office was hardly its nerve centre, but it was an action which followed a pattern of NATO attacks on television newsrooms. During the bombing of Belgrade in the 1999 Kosovo War, a television station was hit.

Today many journalists are convinced that the news media are considered such an important player in war that they are also an unadmitted military target.

Milton and the Birth of Free Speech

Behind these contemporary struggles lies 350 years of conflict about news media freedom. It is a story which not only indicates both the power of the idea of a free press but also its dangers and limitations. Both aspects need to be weighed if we are to understand the debate that surrounds today's news media.

Any potted history must begin with the English Civil War (1642–8), when monarchists and high church types fought republicans and religious dissenters. The war yielded the first great tract in the cause of free expression, John Milton's *Areopagitica* (1644) and its momentous plea: 'Give me the liberty to know, to utter and to argue freely according to conscience, above all liberties.'

Milton's words foreshadowed those of the American Constitution and its First Amendment that: 'Congress shall make no law . . . abridging the freedom of speech or of the press', a hugely important linkage between the primary individual right of free expression and the dominant news medium of the day. Thomas Jefferson reinforced the importance of newspapers when he wrote in 1787 to Colonel Edward Carrington that: 'The basis of our government being the opinion of the people, the very first object should be to keep that right; and were it left to me to decide whether we should have a government without newspapers, or newspapers without a government, I should not hesitate a moment to prefer the latter.'

It is important to remember that these early English and American newspapers were not the first in the world: the media traditions of countries in Asia, Africa, and South America cannot be well understood with narrow reference to the story summarized here. China had official information sheets (*tipao*) centuries before the years of revolution in Europe and America, spawning unofficial rivals of sufficient journalistic enterprise that the Sung dynasty (960–1279) suppressed them. The oldest English-language newspaper still available for physical inspection dates from 1620 and was published in Amsterdam, a major centre of world trade and so an ideal collection and distribution point for news of value to business people. Britain's first national, daily newspaper, published in 1702, was called the *Daily Courant*.

The First Reporters

In England, following the restoration of a monarchy subject to parliamentary authority, pre-publication censorship was abolished, in 1695, opening up a period in which British journalism

Numb.

The Daily Courant.

Wednesday, March 11. 1702.

From the Harlem Courant, Dated March 18. N. S.

Naples, Feb. 22.

ON Wednesday last, our New Viceroy, the Duke of Escalona, arriv'd here with a Squadron of the Galleys of Sicily. He made his Entrance drest in a French habit; and to give us the greater Hopes of the King's coming hither, went to Lodge in one of the little Palaces, leaving the Royal one for his Majesty. The Marquis of Grigni is also arriv'd here with a Regiment of French.

Rome, Feb. 25. In a Military Congregation of State that was held here, it was Resolv'd to draw a Line from Ascoli to the Borders of the Ecclesiastical State, thereby to hinder the Incursions of the Transalpine Troops. Orders are sent to Civita Vecchia to fit out the Galleys, and to strengthen the Garrison of that Place. Signior Casali is made Governor of Perugia. The Marquis del Vasto, and the Prince de Caserta continue still in the Imperial Embassador's Palace; where his Excellency has a Guard of 50 Men every Night in Arms. The King of Portugal has desir'd the Arch-Bishoprick of Lisbon, vacant by the Death of Cardinal Sousa, for the Infante his second Son, who is about 11 Years old.

Vienna, Mar. 4. Orders are sent to the 4 Regiments of Foot, the 2 of Cuirassiers, and to that of Dragoons, which are broke up from Hungary, and are on their way to Italy, and which consist of about 14 or 15000 Men, to hasten their March thither with all Expedition. The 6 new Regiments of Hussars that are now raising, are in so great a forwardness, that they will be compleat, and in a Condition to march by the middle of May. Prince Lewis of Baden has written to Court, to excuse himself from coming thither, his Presence being so very necessary, and so much desir'd on the Upper-Rhine.

Francfort, Mar. 12. The Marquiss d' Uxelles is come to Strasburg, and is to draw together a Body of some Regiments of Horse and Foot from the Garisons of Alsace; but will not lessen those of Strasburg and Landau, which are already very weak. On the other hand, the Troops of His Imperial Majesty, and his Allies, are going to form a Body near Germesheim in the Palatinate, of which Place, as well as of the Lines at Spires, Prince Lewis of Baden is expected to take a View, in three or four days. The English and Dutch Ministers, the Count of Frise, and the Baron Vander Meer, and likewise the Imperial Envoy Count Lowenstein, are gone to Nordlingen, and it is hop'd that in a short time we shall hear from thence of some favourable Resolutions for the Security of the Empire.

Liege, Mar. 14. The French have taken the Cannon de Longie, who was Secretary to the Dean de Mean, out of our Castle, where he has been for some time a Prisoner, and have deliver'd him to the Provost of Maubeuge, who has carry'd him from hence, but we do not know whither.

Paris, Mar. 13. Our Letters from Italy say, That most of our Reinforcements were Landed there; that the Imperial and Ecclesiastical Troops seem to live very peaceably with one another in the Country of Parma, and that the Duke of Vendome, as he was visiting several Posts, was within 100 Paces of falling into the Hands of the Germans. The Duke of Chartres, the Prince of Conti, and several other Princes of the Blood, are to make the Campaign in Flanders under the Duke of Burgundy; and the Duke of Maine is to Command upon the Rhine.

From the Amsterdam Courant, Dated Mar. 18.

Rome, Feb. 25. We are taking here all possible Precautions for the Security of the Ecclesiastical State in this present Conjuncture, and have desir'd to raise 3000 Men in the Cantons of Switzerland. The Pope has appointed the Duke of Berwick to be his Lieutenant-General, and he is to Command 6000 Men on the Frontiers of Naples: He has also settled upon him a Pension of 6000 Crowns a year during Life.

From the Paris Gazette, Dated Mar. 18. 1702.

Naples, Febr. 17. 600 French Soldiers are arrived here, and are expected to be follow'd by 3400 more. A Courier that came hither on the 14th has brought Letters by which we are assur'd that the King of Spain designs to be here towards the end of March; and accordingly Orders are given to make the necessary Preparations against his Arrival. The two Troops of Horse that were Commanded to the Abruzzo are posted at Pescara with a Body of Spanish Foot, and others in the Fort of Montorio.

Paris, March. 18. We have Advice from Toulon of the 5th instant, that the Wind having long stood favourable, 22000 Men were already sail'd for Italy, that 2500 more were Embarking, and that by the 15th it was hoped they might all get thither. The Count d' Estrees arriv'd there on the Third instant, and set all hands at work to fit out the Squadron of 9 Men of War and some Fregats, that are appointed to carry the King of Spain to Naples. His Catholick Majesty will go on Board the *Thunderer*, of 110 Guns.

We have Advice by an Express from Rome of the 18th of February, That notwithstanding the pressing Instances of the Imperial Embassadour, the Pope had Condemn'd the Marquis del Vasto to lose his Head and his Estate to be confiscated, for not appearing to Answer the Charge against him of Publickly Scandalizing Cardinal Janson.

ADVERTISEMENT.

IT will be found from the Foreign Prints, which from time to time, as Occasion offers, will be mention'd in this Paper, that the Author has taken Care to be duly furnish'd with all that comes from Abroad in any Language. And for an Assurance that he will not, under Pretence of having Private Intelligence, impose any Additions of feign'd Circumstances to an Action, but give his Extracts fairly and Impartially; at the beginning of each Article he will quote the Foreign Paper from whence 'tis taken, that the Publick, seeing from what Country a piece of News comes with the Allowance of that Government, may be better able to Judge of the Credibility and Fairness of the Relation: Nor will he take upon him to give any Comments or Conjectures of his own, but will relate only Matter of Fact; supposing other People to have Sense enough to make Reflections for themselves.

This Courant (as the Title shews) will be Publish'd Daily: being design'd to give all the Material News as soon as every Post arrives: and is confin'd to half the Compass, to save the Publick at least half the Impertinences, of ordinary News-Papers.

LONDON. Sold by *E. Mallet*, next Door to the *King's-Arms* Tavern at *Fleet-Bridge*.

2. The *Daily Courant*: Regarded as the first British daily newspaper, the *Daily Courant* was launched on 11 March 1702. Like all early newspapers, it filled most of its space with items borrowed or translated from other publications—in the case of the *Daily Courant* chiefly items from continental Europe. The publisher promised to avoid giving readers 'any comments or conjectures of his own . . . supposing other people to have sense enough to make reflections for themselves'.

blossomed, nurturing talents as diverse as those of Daniel Defoe, Joseph Addison, Richard Steele, Jonathan Swift, John Wilkes, and Thomas Paine. As journalism expanded on many fronts, it began to encounter notions of journalistic ethics and professional practice.

Defoe captured in print the methods of the first professional reporters, working the London coffee houses in 1728.

> Persons are employed . . . to haunt coffee houses and thrust themselves into companies where they are not known; or plant themselves at convenient distances to overhear what is said . . . The same persons are employed to scrape acquaintance with the footmen and other servants of the nobility and gentry; or to learn from those knowing and ingenious persons the motions and designs of their lords and masters, with such occurrences as come to the knowledge of those curious and inquisitive gentlemen. The same persons hang and loiter about the publick offices like housebreakers, waiting for an interview with some little clerk or a conference with a door keeper in order to come at a little news, or an account of transactions; for which the fee is a shilling, or a pint of wine.

It is striking how little has changed in the subsequent 300 years; compare Janet Malcolm's denunciation of the modern journalist as 'confidence man' committed to instinctive treachery cited in the Introduction with Defoe's metaphor of the journalist as burglar. Defoe himself knew much about double-dealing, having worked in espionage, a trade which has much in common with journalism and for which journalism has frequently provided a cover.

Journalism, already in tension with itself about its methods, would be engulfed in battle with the state. Having abandoned the weapon of direct, pre-publication censorship, the British government turned to taxation, in the form of a stamp duty, designed to prevent newspapers becoming too popular and to mark out the respectable from the unrespectable. A more blatant technique was to pay journalists retainers in order to induce them to write more favourable copy. Meanwhile, the libel laws evolved to punish newspapers guilty of defamation or, occasionally, the more serious criminal offence of 'seditious libel'.

In this nascent democracy, the press acquired a unique position, locating itself physically in Fleet Street, between London's business district to the east and Parliament to the west. When the press found itself in conflict with the authorities, it would then, as now, appeal to public opinion or, in the language of the time, 'the London mob'. Large sections of the early press were umbilically tied to the aspirations of their readers for a more democratic society.

Wilkes, Paine, and Revolution

The master of mob-appeal was John Wilkes, who launched his newspaper, the *North Briton*, in 1763 with a proclamation that 'The Liberty of the Press is the birthright of a Briton, and is justly esteemed the finest bulwark of the liberties of this country.' Issue number 45 delivered a stinging attack upon the monarchy, which the paper said had 'sunk even to prostitution'. Wilkes received a libel writ and eventually went to jail and then into exile, from where he returned to a huge London street protest, in which his supporters scrawled the number 45 on every public space they could find. In the end Wilkes triumphed and became a Member of Parliament. Thus did the early English press root its claims and privileges in the soil of public opinion.

This was the state of the English press when Thomas Paine, the son of a Norfolk stay-maker, was in his twenties. Paine, during his period as a resident of Lewes and leading member of the Headstrong Club, may even have met Wilkes when the great rabble-rouser visited the Sussex market town in 1770.[3] At this time admiring continental visitors to Britain noticed the growing scale of the press's influence upon ordinary people. Jean Louis de Lolme, in his 1784 book, *The Constitution of England or an Account of the English Government*, noted that 'every man, down to the labourer, peruses them (newspapers) with a sort of eagerness'.[4]

Paine was one of those who lit the fuse that connected a

new radical journalism with the incendiary politics of North America and France. He sailed for Philadelphia in 1774 and two years later published *Common Sense*, a pamphlet setting out the case for American independence from British rule. A best-seller in America, it was also, according to a contemporary report, 'received in France and in all Europe with rapture', being quickly translated into German, French, and Polish.[5] The next year, Paine returned to England and wrote *Rights of Man*, arguing that human beings have a natural right to govern themselves, rather than to be governed by the beneficiaries of inherited title and power. His reward was to be arraigned for treason, whereupon he fled to Paris and was elected a Deputy in the National Convention, before being swept aside by revolutionary factionalism, which led to his imprisonment and almost to his death. Paine then returned to the United States, where he lived out his days on the uneasy borderland between political power and journalism. He died in New York in 1809, refusing with his last breath to express any belief in the divinity of Jesus Christ.

Paine was a pivotal figure, inheritor of an already distinguished tradition of English journalism and a founding father of American and European political or public journalism. In the United States, his role was as an ideas man and a popularizer of the ideas of others; soon the governmental system Jefferson imagined enlightened by its newspapers was strongly established, and journalists disciplined into professional status, grumbled about, but no threat to the state itself. Paine played with various official governmental roles, but he remained, essentially, an outsider.

In Paris, radical journalism left deeper and bloodier footprints. The French Revolution was, in the view of one media scholar, journalism's 'big bang',[6] in the sense that it brought newspapers and individual journalists into positions of unprecedented influence, at the very centre of public life, as analysts, commentators, agitators, and political actors. In revolutionary France, journalism was literally a matter of life and death. Journalists were consigned to the guillotine, just as their own published words were capable of bestowing a similar fate upon others. The editor of the *Ami du Peuple*, Jean Paul Marat, was murdered in his bath, leaving for posterity a copy of his newspaper stained with his own blood.

The journalistic lesson of the French Revolution is that at moments of national crisis, journalists often find themselves torn between their professional role as detached observers of events and their engagement as activitists. According to the historian Jack Richard Censer, the French radical newspapermen 'generally saw themselves as politicians with a primary responsibility to influence the course of events and with little allegiance toward any abstract journalistic ethic'.[7] Mitchell

Stephens, another press historian, noting the stifling censorship deployed by the official Parisian media in 1789, makes a wider point:

> The French Revolution provides evidence not only of the anti-authoritarian power of news in the hands of a subculture of disenfranchised journalists but of the anti-authoritarian power of the absence of reliable vehicles for news. No news may actually be more destabilising than bad news. Might a couple of accurate, widely distributed newspapers have saved Louis XVI's head?

Or, put another way, a professionalized news media, working to high standards of independence, is crucial to stable, democratic government.

Two Mills on Liberty

This was essentially the view of the Scots utilitarian thinker James Mill, who in 1811 produced an influential essay in which he argued that the dangers of a timorous press, too friendly to established political power, greatly exceeded the political dangers of its opposite. Mill thought the relative political stability of England, Holland, Switzerland, and the United States, compared with the bloody turmoil in France, resulted not from an excessively free press in France, but from an excessively controlled one.

It was not the abuse of a free press which was witnessed during the French revolution; it was the abuse of an enslaved press. . . . Had real freedom of the press been enjoyed—had the honest men whom France contained been left a channel by which to lay their sentiments before the public—had a means been secured of instructing the people in the real nature of the delusions which were practised upon them, the enormities of the revolution would have been confined within a narrow compass, and its termination would have been very different.[8]

Nearly half a century later, James Mill's son, the philosopher John Stuart Mill, set out in eloquent and commanding detail the argument for a society based upon free expression in his 1859 essay *On Liberty*. Mill argued that free expression is fundamental not only to political freedom, but to society's ability to gather knowledge empirically and so to progress scientifically and in any other domain. In a justly famous passage, he writes:

The peculiar evil of silencing an expression of opinion is that it is robbing the human race; posterity as well as the existing generation; those who dissent from the opinion, still more than those who hold it. If the opinion is right, they are deprived of the opportunity of exchanging error for truth: if wrong, they lose, what is almost as great a benefit, the clearer perception and livelier impression of truth, produced by its collision with error.[9]

Mill's views continue to be highly influential, especially among those mistrustful of the power of the state, who are usually called liberals in Europe and libertarians or sometimes, confusingly, Republican conservatives, in the United States.

By the time of *On Liberty*, one of the last explicit state burdens upon newspapers, the stamp duty, had just been abolished, paving the way for the rapid industrialization of a press increasingly dependent upon advertising markets. Newspaper publishers now struggled to reconcile the pressures to increase circulations, reduce unit costs, and attract advertising on the one hand, with the pursuit of a political agenda on the other. With dozens of titles competing for the reader's attention, publishers recognized that they must sugar the political pill.

The Rabble Just Wants to Have Fun

Henry Hetherington was, like Wilkes, a hero of the radical British press. When he launched the *Poor Man's Guardian* in 1831, it was with this uncompromising political message: 'It is the cause of the rabble we advocate, the poor, the suffering, the industrious, the productive classes. . . . We will teach this rabble their power—we will teach them that they are your master, instead of being your slaves.' Like Wilkes, Hetherington spent substantial stints in jail, as did his vendors and other associates, for refusing to pay newspaper stamp duty. Rather than the red stamp of officialdom, his paper carried a logo which declared: 'Knowledge is power. Published in defiance of the law, to try the power of Right against Might.'

Yet only two years after the launch of *Poor Man's Guardian*, Hetheringon was also promising readers of his *Twopenny Dispatch* a diet of 'murders, rapes, suicides, burnings, maimings, theatricals, races, pugilism and . . . every sort of devilment that will make it sell.'[10] Hetherington's recognition that he would need to deploy populist techniques to win support for his political ideas has been fundamental to the success of popular newspapers. Here is the essence of what we have come to call tabloid journalism. There is nothing new in it, or in other apparently recent preoccupations, such as the search for women readers through the use of 'soft' features. In 1693, a broadsheet called the *Ladies Mercury* was launched, promising to answer 'the nice and curious questions concerning love, marriage, behaviour, dress and humour of the female sex, whether virgins, wives or widows'.[11]

When stamp duty was finally abolished in 1855, advertising-funded papers with a wide appeal proved too strong for their more specialized, and mostly duller, subscription-funded political rivals, many of which went out of business. According to some historians, advertising had already established itself as, in effect, 'a new licensing system',[12] designed 'to ensure that the press played an effective role in engineering consent from the lower classes for the social order being established by capitalism'.[13]

Before long, the bigger newspapers, fat with advertising, were trumpeting the glories of a 'new journalism', which the Victorian critic Matthew Arnold loftily dismissed as 'feather-brained', in a pre-run of today's arguments about media 'dumbing down'. These commercial newspapers may have lacked the radical diversity of the earlier political titles, but they were not short of professional ambition. In 1852, *The Times* defined its purpose: 'to obtain the earliest and most correct intelligence of the events of the time and instantly, by disclosing them, to make them the common property of the nation.' The journalist's job, like the historian's, was 'to seek out the truth, above all things, and to present to his readers not such things as statecraft would wish them to know, but the truth as near as he can attain it'.[14] By now, papers like *The Times* were supported by the even more instantaneous information of the first news agencies. Julius Reuter had established his news agency in 1851. A century later, Reuters would be a global organization, with a major presence in information systems for financial markets.

Government by Journalism

The embodiment of the Victorian New Journalism was W. T. Stead, editor of the *Pall Mall Gazette*, who specialized in controversial exposures of sex rackets, as a result of which he too found himself in jail. It was in Holloway Prison, in 1886, that Stead wrote a remarkable essay on the future of journalism, informing the world that journalism had now become 'superior to that of any other institution or profession known among men'. For Stead, the journalist was the key to comprehending public opinion, 'to be both eye and ear for the community'. He concluded: 'I have not yet lost faith in the possibility of some of our great newspaper proprietors who will content himself with a reasonable fortune, and devote the surplus of his gigantic profits to the development of his newspapers as an engine of social reform and as a means of government.'

A means of government? Stead was not kidding. Through 'an exhaustive interrogation of public opinion', such a newspaper would acquire an authority which politicians would be unable to ignore.

> The journalist would speak with an authority far superior to that possessed by any other person; for he would have been the latest to interrogate the democracy. Parliament has attained its utmost development. There is need of a new representative method, not to supersede but to supplement that which exists—a system which will be more elastic, more simple, more direct and more closely in contact with the mind of the people. . . . When the time does arrive, and the man and the money

are both forthcoming, government by journalism will no longer be a somewhat hyperbolic phrase, but a solid fact.[15]

This early techno-utopianism foreshadows not only today's alarms about 'government by the media' and declining affiliation to institutions of representative democracy but also some of the more adventurous claims made 150 years later for the internet, which Californian visionaries would claim to be a means not only of unsurpassed human communication, but in its networking of global human intelligence, technology's contribution to the metaphysical task of knowing the mind of God.[16]

Stead's hubris about journalism was consistent with the optimism of Victorian Britain. The country became more prosperous as the reach of empire extended, creating openings for newspapers not with soberly descriptive names such as *The Times*, *The Gazette*, and *The Record*, but with ablaze with aspiration: the *Mirror*, the *Sun*, the *Comet*, and the *Star*. Most of Britain's great popular newspapers of today were born in the final years of Victoria's reign: the *Daily Mail* (1896), the *Daily Express* (1900), and the *Daily Mirror* (1903), while in the United States proprietors like William Randolph Hearst and Joseph Pulitzer were creating the 'yellow' press.

Electronic Media Monopolies

The heyday of the market-based, industrialized free press was, however, remarkably short. Within a couple of decades of the new century, the market-based model for the development of news media came under challenge, first from radio, then from television and, towards the end of the twentieth century, from the internet. These were media which would soon acquire a reach never achieved by newspapers and they were born not in tiny printers' shops subject to the laws of a market economy; rather, they were inventions naturally and speedily commandeered by governments, which took the view that the new communications technologies must be owned or licensed by the state. It is too easily forgotten that the media technologies of the twentieth century have their roots not in markets, but in monopoly or licensed oligopoly.

From the point of view of journalism, this is a critical point of distinction because news, information, and advertising would no longer be a product of societies based largely upon market economics, still struggling towards basic democracy. The twentieth century's new information economy had as its background the rise of communism and fascism, that took a very different ideological view of the ownership and responsibilities of news media.

The twenty-first century information or knowledge economy,

following the collapse of the Berlin Wall in 1989 and the decisive reverse of communism, would arise from electronic news technologies that again promised, as in the heyday of the press, low entry cost and unchecked freedom of distribution. But it was by no means clear whether the mass medium of television, which remained potent and more influential than any other news medium, would itself become more like the relatively unregulated market for newspapers, or whether perhaps newspapers, as they developed screen-based, electronic formats themselves, would become more like broadcasting. Or, put another way: would the eighteenth-century settlement on free expression and free newspapers hold good? How would journalism adapt its own changed place in politics and public life and its own relationship with an ever more media-aware audience?

Old Media Never Die

What is clear is that the story of the news media involves a process of evolution, in which old media are not replaced by new media, but modified by them. The same can be said for the legal framework within which media operate: it is in a state of constant adaptation. Roger Fidler, an authority on new media, calls this the principle of 'co-evolution and co-existence', which states that: 'All forms of communication media co-exist and co-evolve within an expanding, complex adaptive system. As each new form emerges and develops, it influences, over time and to varying degrees, the development of every other existing form.'[17] Thus the printed page delivered a framework for order, argument, and the deployment of evidence. News could be recounted in some detail, because it could be read and reread at leisure, but it also acquired a formal, public stature. Those who could not read had the news read to them in public places. Societies developed an idea of what constitutes 'the news' or 'the news of the day'. Armed with a grammar of headlines and column layout, newspapers could declare priorities, balance light and shade, and establish personality. As the technology for mass reproduction of pictures became available, each one 'worth a thousand words', image and text were able to work in counterpoint and to stir emotions. In the best popular newspapers, like *Picture Post*, the images themselves would tell powerful stories, opening up a new field of photo-journalism, where photography led the process of journalistic discovery.

With radio, the initial instinct was to pursue the stiff template of print journalism; in France, the first radio newsreels were called '*gazettes parlées*', spoken newspapers. But soon radio too identified its natural advantages of immediacy and conversational familiarity, the fact that its reporters could demonstrate their presence at the news scene by recording and broadcasting 'actuality'. As media multiplied and technologies

3. Winston Churchill. A master of radio, via which Churchill delivered his famous wartime broadcasts, he was less keen on television, which he described as a 'peep show'. News on both radio and television was, in effect, licensed by governments, in contrast with the press, which had its origin in free, commercial markets.

advanced, radio also discovered that it had a great advantage in that it could be used or enjoyed while the listener engaged in other activities, such as driving a car, or even consuming other media.

Television was assailed from its inception as a superficial thing. Winston Churchill called it a 'peep show' and many have argued that it is doomed to trivialize all it touches. But, in fact, television brought unprecedented authority to news, along with a repertoire of tricks from the entertainment business. The evidential quality of a moving picture (seeing is believing) proved superior, certainly in terms of a mass audience, to the most finely marshalled evidence in the most measured prose. The televised interview, by conveying the facial and body language of the interviewee, was able to operate at a richer and more convincing level than its newspaper equivalent.

With on-line media, the key journalistic innovation to date has been interactivity between the news provider and the audience, which may promise some levelling out the relationship between the supplier and consumer of news. On-line media also frequently supply their users with further sources of information, via hyperlinks, which is another way in which the authority of the news provider shifts, becoming in effect a networker of a variety of news sources, rather than the undisputed bearer of 'the news' or 'the truth.' In this way, news technologies have

4. Tiananmen Square. Television has been frequently attacked for 'dumbing down' the news media, but when big events unfold, there is nothing to compare with the memorable drama of television news. Here, a student demonstrator halts a column of tanks in Tiananmen Square, during the famous protests in 1989.

both reflected and stimulated a more relativistic view of what constitutes 'the truth' or 'objective fact.'

The Asian Model

These changes in technology are themselves also deeply contingent upon the prevailing political and cultural climate in different countries. Singapore,[18] for example, is a tiny city-state, which has successfully put itself at the forefront of the latest information technology, while pursuing what it sees as an 'Asian model' of democracy, namely one that involves explicit acts of censorship by the state, aimed at ensuring that the 'wrong' kind of news reporting does not undermine social and racial harmony, political stability, and economic advance. In recent years, a number of prominent Western publications, including *The Economist* and the *Wall Street Journal*, have been banned or restricted in Singapore.

The modern Japanese press, by contrast, enjoys the protection of a national constitution which enshrines the principle of press freedom, established under strong American influence after the Second World War, and is not subject to state censorship. But the workings of Japanese news media are barely recognizable to journalists from the United States or Britain. They arise, perhaps, from the fact that Japan is still a relatively young democracy, but more significantly from a difference in the way that Japanese organizations and interests negotiate with each other and reach agreement. Japanese journalists, for example, are bound together in a network of a thousand 'press clubs', all linked to major institutional or industrial sources of power and therefore of news, and designed to ensure that both sides play by a set of unofficial rules. This is, in essence, a form of self-regulation, designed to avoid embarrassment and misunderstanding, but which in the opinion of its critics neuters and homogenizes Japan's journalism through the management of 'an unchallenged monopoly on the flow of news or any other form of information'.[19]

To Western critics, the system is, like other Japanese institutional practices, conservative, secretive, and non-confrontational to the point where it represents an impediment to social and political progress, preventing journalism from doing its job of exposing conflicting interests and facts. This, however, was a view much less stridently expressed in the 1970s and early 1980s, when Japanese manufacturing industry was carrying all before it, based apparently upon a distinctive Japanese culture of cooperation and conflict-avoidance. Perhaps Japan's distinctive contribution to consumer culture bears some relation to its unique system of press management.

Vive la France

Even within Western Europe, there are significant differences in the culture and practice of journalism, and therefore in the practical meaning of 'press freedom'. France, for example, has a statutory law to protect privacy, along with a culture in which exposure of personal relationships is not regarded as the staple diet of even the most popular journalism. Anglo-Saxon critics of these arrangements say that they allow personal dishonesty even at the highest political level to go unchallenged. Defenders retort that the British press suffers from a juvenile obsession with stories about bonking soap opera stars and love-rat melodramas.

Regulation: Economics versus Culture

For governments, however, the digital technologies that are making journalism global in its scope and bringing about the convergence of broadcasting and print, computers and telecommunications, raise pressing questions. Should they, can they, retain barriers to the entry of non-nationals into ownership of news media? Can they, in the world of the internet, continue to enforce curbs on material offensive to public taste and decency? Is it possible for politicians to continue to require that licensed broadcasters supply only news which is accurate and politically impartial, at a time when broadcasters can transmit their material via telephone lines, as well as through the licensed broadcast spectrum? Today, it is difficult to tell apart the internet productions of newspapers, which are essentially unregulated, from those of broadcasters, which are mostly rather heavily regulated.

Governments are also torn about their priorities on media policy. They want their media and communications industries to perform well in economic terms, to boost the 'knowledge economy', which argues for greater deregulation, but they also want to defend cultural, social, and political interests, which argues for continued regulation. Some have reached the conclusion that the best way forward is to bring together the regulatory bodies which have grown up over the years in different media into a united force responsible for everything from the allocation of radio spectrum to its many users (ranging across military radar systems, mobile phones, and television) to the supervision of 'public service' or 'public interest' agreements with licensed broadcasters using that spectrum. It remains to be seen how successful such reforms will be.

It is hardly surprising, in these circumstances, that John Stuart Mill's idea of 'liberty' in publishing is contested. We live in more chastened times. As George Orwell said in his 1946 essay, *The Prevention of Literature*: 'the controversy over freedom of speech and of the press is at bottom a controversy over the desirability, or otherwise, of telling lies. What is really at issue is the right to report contemporary events truthfully, or as truthfully as is consistent with the ignorance, bias and self-deception from which every observer necessarily suffers.' Orwell understood better than most that governments, along with other powerful institutions, would continue to deploy a formidable array of impediments to the trouble-free pursuit of this ambition and that journalism's challenge would be to see beyond

5. George Orwell was probably the twentieth century's greatest journalist. Not only did he write brilliantly and didactically about the art of clear writing, he also, in his novels *Animal Farm* and *1984*, imagined a dystopia in which the corruption of information systems would lead to tyranny and systematic violence. Today, Orwell's Big Brother has taken on a more playful meaning, in reality television.

these interests to create a sphere of public information on which citizens could depend, without themselves forming a new type of bullying authority.

Half a century after Orwell, Adam Michnik, editor-in-chief of *Gazeta Wyborcza*, and veteran of the struggle to democratize Poland, set out ten commandments for the revived journalism of his own country. The first declared:

> Our God, who led us out from bondage has two names: Freedom and Truth. To this God we subordinate ourselves completely. If we bow to other gods—the state, the nation, the family, public security—at the expense of Freedom and Truth, we shall be punished with the loss of reliability. Without reliability, one cannot be a journalist.[20]

Yet maps attempting to show the state of world press freedom still show only a minority of the world's land mass (North America, Europe, India, Australasia, and small parts of Africa) as enjoying a high level of news media freedom. Latin America, Russia, and parts of Central Europe are regarded as partly free, with most of Africa, the Middle East, and China decidedly not free. Anthony Collings, an American newsman and commentator on movements for independent journalism around the world, takes a broadly optimistic view, arguing that the persistence of reasonable levels of press freedom in Hong Kong may indicate that China is moving uneluctably in the direction of greater publishing freedom. 'Armed conflict aside, the factors favourable for press freedom remain strong at the outset of the twenty-first century, factors that include western influence, the spread of democracy, the rise of the internet and expanding global trade.'[21] Given the West's commitment to all of these political, cultural, economic, and technological changes, it is ironic that American journalism, based in the world's most marketized economy, should be under such strong critical assault from within. It suggests that continued progress towards the idea of greater news media freedom and democracy will be more complex than the rhetoric of Western campaigners sometimes suggests. The relationship between journalism and the state is never stable, in any type of society but in advanced democracies, where the authority of the state is under threat from global economic and technological forces, journalism must ask itself more searching questions about the 'public interst' it claims to represent.

2

Big Brother

Journalism and the State

In December 2001 I spent some time in Russia, talking to journalists from the length and breadth of that vast country. They had come together for the annual media seminar of the Moscow School of Political Studies, one of many bodies formed in the early years of glasnost to help disseminate ideas and good practice from democratic societies.

At one level, such evangelism can only be unreservedly welcomed. No one can defend the deceitful propaganda of the 'information regimes' of the Soviet era, when the titles of leading newspapers such as *Pravda* ('Truth') were turned into grim self-parodies. Yet, as I sat through the seminar, I couldn't avoid a sense of irony at the high-flown and moralizing rhetoric of the evangelists at a time when Western journalism, American journalism especially, is widely felt to be in trouble, a victim of the effects of shareholder ownership, corporate greed, and diminished civic purpose. In 2002, as stock markets collapsed amid wave after wave of corporate scandal, it was by no means obvious that advanced capitalism's model of lightly regulated big business as the answer to almost everything offered a healthy repository for the traditions of free news media.

The pro-market rhetoric I have in mind reached its high point in the 1980s and the 1990s, when President Reagan defined his country's cold war antagonist as 'the evil empire' and American capital, technology, and cultural reach appeared beyond challenge. Nowhere was this spirit more ambitiously stated than in the speeches of Rupert Murdoch, the Australian who adopted American citizenship in order to pursue his ambition of owning US television interests. This is how Murdoch described the arrival in Europe of multi-channel satellite television in 1989 in a speech to television executives in Edinburgh. 'In 1694, the English Parliament abolished pre-publication censorship of the printing presses,' Murdoch told his audience, 'leaving the printed word solely to the general laws of the land, an event described by that great Whig historian, Macaulay, as greater in its contribution to English liberty than either the Magna Carta or the Bill of Rights. I believe that British television has now begun its own 1694.'[1] Four years later, in another speech, this time in London, Murdoch declared that the new communications technologies 'have proved an unambiguous threat to totalitarian regimes everywhere. . . . Satellite broadcasting makes it possible for information-hungry residents of many closed societies to by-pass state-controlled television channels.'[2] This was the spirit which saw news entrepreneurs like Murdoch's great rival Ted Turner, founder of the news network CNN, embark for

Moscow in the early 1990s, convinced that their proposed new channels would both liberate their viewers and enrich their owners.

Russian Journalism at the Edge

By the first years of the new millennium, the situation looked a good deal more complicated. Here at a Soviet-era conference centre on the edge of snow-bound Moscow, senior figures from the Russian Parliament, the Duma, the state television authorities, and the Moscow press squared up to a group of young, but by no means inexperienced journalists from across Russia: from Siberia to the east and Stavropol to the south and from Moscow and St Petersburg at the old, imperial centre. At issue was the kind of journalism developing in Russia, as it struggles between the dizzying polarities of anarcho-capitalism and fading memories of Soviet certainty.

Irina Lukyanova, a former newspaper journalist was at that time presenter of the main political current affairs programme of SkaT, a television station in Samara, in the Volga. I asked her what influence she had over who appeared on her show—the kind of issue often hotly contested in the West between producers and presenters. 'I am allowed to choose,' she replied, 'except for those who pay for their places.' Those who pay? 'Yes, there are usually a couple of seats for those who pay, mainly politicians or business people.' How much do they pay? 'About a thousand US dollars. The price is set by the advertising department.' A further indignity, she explained, was the role demanded of journalists like her during election periods by the powerful regional politicians who, along with business tycoons, have taken control of much of Russia's political life in the post-Soviet period. Journalists are pressured to work for the election campaign teams where, inside a few weeks, they can earn as much as in the rest of the year. Around election time, Irina, who is popular with her audience, said she was required to act as 'interviewer' for what in effect were party-political broadcasts—a clear conflict of roles. She had dealt with this situation by developing a 'cold and mechanical' style of interviewing for these occasions, the stance of a 'microphone holder' rather than a journalist. I asked her to demonstrate, using a spoon as a microphone. It was an impressively coded statement against a practice she bitterly resented, but which she felt she could not change.

In the newspaper world, life can be even tougher. Alexander Yakhontov was editor of a weekly paper, *Novaya Gazeta*, in a small city a few hundred miles south of Moscow. He made a start in journalism in 1991, during the warm spring which followed the ending of the cold war. Like most papers, *Novaya Gazeta* had begun life as a tiny cog in the Community Party machine—the voice of the local Young Communist League. In its communist heyday, it recorded a meaningless, but impressive-sounding circulation figure of 50,000. Reborn, post-glasnost, as a title owned by its staff with what Yakhontov styles a 'public watchdog' role in its community largely learnt from American example, the paper was by the end of 2001 struggling to sell 4,000 copies a week and had been subject to repeated bouts of harassment from the local governor. Official tactics included efforts to evict the paper from its offices, court action, and, for a period, the establishment of a rival paper with an almost identical name. When I asked Alexander Yakhontov about his hopes for the future, he replied: 'The intelligentsia needs independent opinion. I hope we shall survive, despite all the hardships.'

The world knows little of the lives of journalists like Irina Lukyanova and Alexander Yakhontov, but their stories are a reminder that the struggle for journalism to define its relationship with the state continues, in very different ways in different places, and often amid great hardship. For these proponents of the 'new journalism' of modern Russia, this is not a time of revolutionary optimism, as in the America of 1776, or even the bloody, adrenalin-fuelled factionalism of France in 1790; it is a long, exhausting journey on a road already deeply potholed by imploded ideals and fractured expectations. Russia is building its democracy and a tradition of freedom for its news media not in the nascent markets of early capitalism, as happened in Europe and North America, but amid the ruins of state socialism, and in the age of electronic media. In the Soviet Union, as in many other places, the news media were under the direct control of the state. In modern Russia, the renegotiation of the relationship between the new journalism and the reformed state has centred on the issue of television.

Russia's TV Wars

During that same trip, I visited the huge Ostankino broadcasting complex on the edge of Moscow to meet some of the people at the centre of the battle for control of the now partially privatized Russian television system. A few weeks earlier one group of journalists had walked out of the country's third largest network, NTV, in order to set up shop on the other side of the complex with the rival TV6, which was later forced off the air-waves. This contest, depending upon your informant, demonstrated that the Kremlin was still fixing television industry politics at the highest level or that the Kremlin was gradually handing power to competing business interests, themselves heavily politically connected.[3] I was struck by the contrast between what I saw in the NTV news production suite that evening and what I had observed fourteen years earlier, when I had visited Ostankino as the head of a BBC News delegation to

Gostelradio, then the monopoly Soviet broadcaster, just before the fall of the Berlin Wall. Arriving then at about 11 a.m., I was asked whether I would like to observe the rehearsals for that evening's main television news bulletin, which was to be read by a thick-set man in a shiny suit. 'How can you rehearse a bulletin so long before it goes on air, since you can't yet know what the main news items will be?' I enquired. 'We already have our script. It has been cleared,' my host replied. In Soviet Russia, breaking news conformed to the working patterns of bureaucrats. As usual, it began with an account of a visit to Moscow by a sympathetic foreign dignitary.

The atmosphere at NTV at the start of the new millennium was very distant from this. Not only had the dress code changed—I don't recall young women in tight leather trousers in 1988—but so too had the news selection. On the evening of my visit, NTV led with a reheated allegation of Kremlin involvement in the bombing of a Moscow apartment block, which triggered, or had been used to justify, escalation of the war in Chechnya. This war, between the Russian state and a separatist movement, presented a huge challenge to emerging media freedoms in Russia, exemplified when Russian troops handed over Andrei Babitsky, a Russian journalist working for the US government-funded Radio Liberty, to rebel troops. President Putin had described Babitsky's reporting as 'much more dangerous than firing a machine gun'.[4] As I entered the NTV newsroom, the first computer screen I saw displayed the Drudge Report, the American muck-raking internet site. That same day, revelations about sexual misdemeanours by an executive involved in the TV6–NTV row would appear on a Russian website specializing in what Russians call 'compromat'—sleaze. This may not be a utopia of free expression, but it is a very long way from the old *Pravda*, with its global network of dull writers trained to eat well and service the party line.

Journalism in Moscow today has many faults, but it is, at least, no longer homogeneous. There are good papers, which challenge official thinking, as well as lively television current affairs and radio talk shows. But it is also brittle, as a public relations company demonstrated in September 2001, when it offered newspaper editors a fee to publicize the opening of a non-existent hi-fi shop. Of the twenty-one titles approached, thirteen obliged.[5] It is fair to say, as Frank Ellis has pointed out, that Russia's media laws are, on paper, as liberal as those of any Western country. But changing cultures, and working out a plausible, robust relationship between journalists and the power of the state, or of business, will not follow any easy formula from the other side of the world. 'Russian journalists are slowly and surely habituating themselves to working in an arena of rights and responsibilities,' says Ellis, in which juridical persons can be held accountable for breaches of the law. If, to the Western eye Russian media legislation and judicial process smacks of the American Wild West, then this is not entirely unexpected. The rule of law, and the importance of contract and civic self-discipline do not come ready-made. . . . Real-existing socialism totally destroyed civil society.'[6]

This last point is crucial. Freedom for the news media has very seldom been conceded by the state without a fight and its maintenance does indeed depend upon the institutions of civil society, the institutional activities of free citizens. This category includes business, but it also encompasses pressure groups, professional societies, consumer organizations, trade unions, and ad hoc demonstrators. When the US Congress during the Clinton presidency passed a law restricting communication on the internet, on the grounds of protecting the public from indecent material, the Supreme Court struck the law down on the grounds that the Communications Decency Act infringed the First Amendment. In free societies, the Court indicated, journalism belongs to the people as a whole, not to their rulers. But for this arrangement to flourish, journalism needs, in all its diversity, to maintain widespread and deeply rooted popular support.

American Self-Doubt

What, then, is to be made of the clamour from within Western journalism about its decline into celebrity-worship, sensation, inaccuracy, and commoditization at the hands of a new generation of proprietors? Could it be true, as an anti-capitalism protestor put it on May Day 2002: 'we have defeated communism and fascism—now we must defeat corporatism.'

In recent years, there has been a flood of American books and articles denouncing the excessive commercialization of the US news industry, its corruption by over-reliance upon advertising, and its increasingly damaging association with the corporate interests of its owners. The flavour of the position is captured in the title of one of the earliest of these critiques, James Fallows's '*Breaking the News: How the Media Undermine American Democracy*.' Fallows made his name with this tract and went on to edit the news weekly, *US News and World Report*. Another example is *Trivia Pursuit*,[7] a 1998 book by Knowlton Nash, a well-known Canadian broadcaster. Its subtitle is: *How Showbiz Values are Corrupting the News*.' Arthur E. Rowse, a journalist who has served on the *Washington Post* and the *Boston Globe*, entitled his confessional: *Drive-by Journalism: The Assault on Your Need to Know*.[8] Rowse consciously harks back to the traditional values of 'old journalism' as an antidote to the new variety, which is perceived by many American newspaper people to have infected not only television, but also the newer, on-line media. According to Rowse, the crimes of the 'new news' people are that they have corrupted journalism with reckless mergers, 'exploited the First Amendment for profit', trivialized coverage of politics and public life and become over reliant on publicists rather than reporting skills. The American public watchdog, say the critics, has rotten teeth. Rowse's book is dedicated to 'all the journalists still fighting to free the news business from itself', Nash's to 'the foot soldiers of journalism who tell it like it is'.

The First Amendment Traduced

The most striking charge is that the First Amendment, designed to guarantee the individual's right to free expression, along with the press's right to share that freedom, has been hijacked in pursuit of commercial interests. The argument is that the First Amendment is fundamentally intended to protect the individual right of free expression, not the corporate interests of a Disney Corporation or AOL–Time Warner, which is in business to enhance shareholder value. Or, put another way, if the corporation's self-interest can be shown to be incompatible with the values of citizen's or public journalism, dedicated to holding power to account, the First Amendment can no longer be viewed as an unbreachable defence of journalism.

This argument has been advanced vigorously by the

Committee of Concerned Journalists. Its manifesto warns of[9] 'a fundamental and epic change with enormous implications for democratic society'.[10] When the authors map the crisis in American journalism, they find that the public is reading less news, watching less news, and feeling less trust in journalists and journalism. In short, public confidence in the American Constitution has been shaken.

Public Journalism Fights Back

One envisaged remedy for this state of affairs is a return to 'public journalism', sometimes called 'civic journalism', which emphasizes the importance of journalists working more closely within their communities and where possible taking responsibility for more than their reporting. For example, a local newspaper might put itself at the service of a programme of environmental improvement, or a drive for higher standards in local schools, using not only the conventional tactics of revelatory reporting and setting out of opinions, but also through more deliberately constructive interventions: the dissemination of public information material, running competitions, working with schools, and so on. Public journalism seeks to widen news agendas, beyond the familiar territory of crime, social disorder, and entertainment. Fallows's book also calls for higher personal standards among American journalists, who are urged to declare their financial and other interests, from the lecture circuit and commercial consultancy, in the way that politicians must. All of this is aimed at countering an image which, the reformers say, has turned many of the country's best-known journalists from 'muck-rakers into buck-rakers'.

Public journalism, however, has attracted some powerful enemies within journalism. They argue that public journalism risks distorting the role of the journalist as an independent watchdog against power, and especially against governmental misbehaviour, by turning journalists into developers of policy and shapers of public opinion and so distracting reporters from their true mission of reporting without fear or favour. Among the critics is Leonard Downie, executive editor of the *Washington Post.* Downie is a journalist so committed to the principle of journalistic detachment from civic life that he refuses even to cast a secret vote in elections on the grounds that this might corrupt the impartiality of his editorial judgement. But Downie himself has contributed something to the atmosphere of apocalypse in his own book, co-written with fellow *Washington Post* senior correspondent Robert G. Kaiser, and subtitled '*American Journalism in Peril*'.[11] It echoes the catalogue of woes arising from the cutbacks in newsroom budgets, corporate mergers, the trivialization of network television news, and diminished public engagement with news, but also insists that 'America's best news organizations became stronger in the nineties than they had ever been.' Yet, by the early years of the decade, even august papers like the *Post*, the *New York Times*, and the *Wall Street Journal* were being battered by the combined forces of a serious advertising downturn and the results of their own miscalculations about investment in on-line news services. 'Too many once-distinguished news organizations have lost their lustre; too few new ones have materialized,' say Downie and Kaiser. The motivations of the 'public journalists' to reconnect with community, or a public sphere less subject to wholesale commercialism, surely have something to contribute to addressing this sorry state of affairs.

Who's to Blame? Send for the Regulator

There are a number of reasons why this debate has flared so vividly in North America, of which the most benign is the fact that the US has a strong tradition of debate about journalistic issues, based upon its constitutional commitment to free news media and its unrivalled network of journalism schools and media think tanks, many of them endowed by organizations which cheerfully combined muck-raking and buck-raking in less self-critical times.

But in the context of understanding the changing relationship between journalism and the state, the more significant reason for American journalism's era of self-doubt is the growth in corporate media power, which is discussed further in Chapter 4. This is a complex subject, frequently distorted by over-simplification in media discussion, but there is no doubting that in the United States, the authorities responsible for regulating electronic communication, and thus the governmental carriers of American constitutional values in this vital part of the news media, have taken an increasingly liberal or deregulatory stance. Although the US Federal Communications Commission never pursued strongly stated public service obligations for broadcasting in the European manner, it began, during the Reagan presidency, to withdraw from any attempt to apply 'public interest' or 'fairness' considerations to television news services. The result was diminished incentive for the networks to cross-subsidize their mostly non-profit-making news divisions, which had benefited previously from what NBC's long-serving presenter, Tom Brokaw, has called 'conscience money'.[12] This is certainly one important factor, if not the central explanation, why American network television news has become increasingly the prisoner of an entertainment ratings cultures: building its bulletins around shorter items and a more parochial news agenda. None of these trends have occurred to anything like the same extent in Europe.[13]

Convergence in the technologies of telecommunications,

broadcasting, and computers is today obliging everyone to rethink the structure of their regulatory arrangements. Britain is among those to have decided that the best approach (like the American) is to have a single point of regulatory authority for all systems of electronic communication, something which has obliged UK politicians to readdress the place of news within that system of statutory regulation. Should they, following the Rupert Murdoch argument, withdraw from regulation and leave television, radio, and on-line journalism to follow the path of newspapers, determined by commercial market forces? Or will they, noting the relative decline of influence of newspapers, compared with electronic media, defend the idea that there is a public interest at stake here which markets are incapable of protecting to the necessary degree.

At present, for example, most European countries, including the UK, have laws that require television news to be politically impartial, a stricture which applies to any broadcaster seeking a licence to transmit within their territory. Politicians of all parties tend to support this status quo and there is evidence of strong, if diminishing, public support for this type of content regulation.[14] Those less inclined to support the system are those who enjoy the widest range of choice in their television services, through the still relatively new mechanisms of cable and satellite delivery. These are viewers who can receive not only the highly regulated public service news output of the BBC and its regulated commercial rivals, ITV, Channel 4, and Channel 5, but who can also pick up American television news, as well as a host of other services originating beyond the national borders which were until very recently impregnable in broadcasting terms. In Britain, these newcomers include a number of Asian television stations, serving Britain's large Indian, Pakistani, and Bangladeshi population, along with the Arabic-language station, Al Jazeera. Another new player in Britain is Rupert Murdoch's Fox News, created for the American market with the deliberate aim of redressing what its owner sees as the liberal/left tendency in American network news and epitomized by Sky's great global rival, CNN. According to BSkyB, the satellite television company of which Murdoch owns 36 per cent, and which dominates the UK pay television market: 'the time will come when there will be no further need for impartiality rules for any of the media.'[15] This argument is enhanced if we imagine, that television news will also be available via broadband telecommunications networks, as well as by the current range of broadcast technologies.

There can be no denying the power of this vision, nor the fact that Murdoch has pursued it with heavy and mostly well-judged investment around the world. But it is also a vision that has encountered obstacles and self-contradictions. In China, one of the ‘closed societies’ referred to in his 1993 speech, Murdoch successfully bargained with the political authorities for permission to sell a politically sanitized version of his satellite television services, placing business values ahead of Magna Carta values, and ensuring that BBC news was excluded from his China service. In Britain, Murdoch’s many opponents argue that his vision of a wholly market-driven broadcasting system will diminish range and quality because it would, logically, make it impossible to sustain a large, publicly funded organization like the BBC. The fact that Britain has so far been relatively untouched by the self-doubt of American journalism may partly reflect the arrogance of British journalists, which is considerable, but it could also be something to do with the fact that the BBC, in defiance of market forces, is given almost £3bn a year of public money, which enables it to supply a form of high-quality public journalism not only at the level of the UK, but also to localities, regions, and internationally. Mikhail Gorbachev has spoken of the way he depended upon news from the BBC at crucial moments in his own political career and it was from the BBC that Northern Alliance troops in the deserts of Afghanistan got their information in the war against the Taliban in 2002.

No Bonfire of Regulations Tonight

So the global reality in the first years of the twenty-first century was not, as Murdoch had predicted, a bonfire of broadcast regulation. Rather, what we started to see was a cautious lightening of the regulatory burden, aimed at improving investment flows and innovation in electronic communications generally, combined with a continued insistence on the state's right to sanction public investment in non-market-driven broadcasting.

In this respect, the United States is an anomaly, and arguably justifiably so, in the sense that it is the only country with a domestic market large enough to generate serious competition in all branches of broadcasting and electronic communication. In the European Union, it is now established in law that member states have the right to subsidize their broadcasters on public interest grounds, in ways impermissible in most industries. In some countries, notably France, this position reflects a long-standing and passionately articulated resistance to the Americanization of national cultures. This Euro-nationalism was clearly evident during the crisis at the media giant Vivendi in 2002, when the company's boss, Jean Marie-Messier, dubbed by his critics Maître de l'Univers Moi-Même, was evicted following his attempts, in effect, to transplant the company's heart to New York. When, almost simultaneously, the German Kirch Media group got into equally deep trouble, politicians were swift to indicate that they were looking towards some sort of 'German solution' to the problems.

It would be wrong, however, to suggest that Europe has been immune to the pessimism which has characterized America's internal debate about journalism. Across Europe, falling turnout at elections has been linked to the failings of the news media, which are accused somewhat self-contradictorily of both dumbing down and failing to appeal to young people. Audiences to mainstream television news bulletins and to current affairs programmes have fallen steadily in the last decade, along with readership of newspapers. Voting levels in European Union elections fell from two-thirds to under half in the last twenty years and across Europe, there is talk of the 'vanishing young reader' of newspapers.[16] In the British general election of 2002, only 59.4 per cent of those entitled voted, the lowest figure since women got the vote. Among 18 to 25 year olds the figure was 39 per cent. The BBC quickly launched an internal inquiry about its own programmes, debating the premise that 'neither politicians nor media are truly in step with the mood of the nation'.[17] Subsequent research suggested that, from the public's point of view, the cause of these problems lay more at the door of the politicians than the news media, though it is also clear that the British news media do a less good job at reporting local events, compared with national and world events, and that they are failing to engage with the interests of younger people, and especially with the interests of people from Britain's ethnic minority communities.[18]

According to a wide range of critics and scholars, the problems of the European news media are very much of their own making. The French sociologist Pierre Bourdieu's study of television journalism found a system where 'all production is oriented toward preserving established values' and where competition 'rather than generating originality and diversity, tends to favour uniformity',[19] though it is not clear from Bourdieu's argument whether the fault he finds lies chiefly with the market or the pervasive relationship between the French state and the country's electronic news media. What France has, says Serge Halimi, another left-wing critic who writes for *Le Monde Diplomatique*, is 'media which is more and more ubiquitous, journalists who are more and more docile and a public information system which is more and more mediocre'.[20]

The doyen of this leftist critique of journalism as an arm of established power is the American linguist Noam Chomsky, whose writings have had considerable influence upon more popular writers like John Pilger, the Australian campaigning journalist, who has written extensively about the decline of popular journalism. Pilger argues that British television is just as parochial as American television and certainly does not spare the BBC from his characterization of the mass media as a willing tool of a propagandizing political establishment, blind to wider issues of poverty and injustice. In Pilger's assessment, most journalists have become either puppets of tough proprietors like Rupert Murdoch or lazy and largely passive victims of public relations experts.[21] They are pursuing a 'hidden agenda'—sometimes concealed even from journalists themselves. In the extraordinary period following the terrorist attacks on New York and Washington in 2001, Pilger found himself promoted from his habitual pastures in the pages of left-wing magazines and broadsheet newspapers to the front page of the *Daily Mirror*, a traditionally Labour-supporting, mass-selling tabloid, whose editor decided that the outbreak of the war on terrorism justified a change of course from a diet of celebrity news to a campaigning stance strongly critical of the Bush–Blair conduct of the conflict. This led in July 2002 to a front page featuring a Pilger polemic accusing the United States of being 'the world's leading rogue state'.[22]

Journalists at War

War has always delivered a severe test of journalistic independence.

In time of war, journalists face great pressures to aid the war effort and to avoid undermining public morale. Philip Knightley, a journalist and historian of the journalism of war, argues that only in a 'war of national survival',[23] such as the Second World War, should journalists entertain the idea of explicit cooperation with the state. Since most wars are not of this type, being conducted for reasons of geopolitical advantage or even for reasons of domestic politics, he maintains that journalists can and must retain their critical distance. He also concludes that, given the character of modern warfare, and the constraints imposed by the military on war reporting, it has become in effect impossible to do an honest job as a war reporter. 'I predict that control of war correspondents, both open and covert, will be even tighter and that in general this will be accepted by the media, because in wartime it considers its commercial and political interests lie in supporting the government of the day. The age of the war correspondent as hero is clearly over.'[24]

Yet in situations where a newspaper or broadcaster knows that its own readers, or the children of its own readers, are risking their lives in military action, or are in danger at home from terrorism, there is an understandable sensitivity involved which goes beyond crude commercial and political self-interest.

There is no denying that this creates acute ethical conflicts for journalists. In the 1991 Gulf War, for example, the news media prominently reported information about the likely allied counter-invasion of Kuwait, designed by military commanders to confuse the Iraqi enemy. If journalists had known this infor-

6. Saddam Hussain of Iraq invaded Kuwait in 1991, provoking war with the Western powers. The cable news company CNN made its name during the war, with its since much-imitated round the clock coverage.

mation to be wrong, would they still have been right to report it? If a journalist had known the real, secret plan, would it have been correct to report that, even if it meant the loss of many of his own country's soldiers' lives? It is difficult to believe that any journalist or news medium rooted in a national community could answer yes to the second question. But the Gulf War does not qualify as a war of national survival by Knightley's definition.

Journalists clearly do have a responsibility not to fall for brazen propaganda, of the kind the British government used to such advantage during the First World War, circulating stories about German troops massacring babies and slicing the breasts from women as they advanced into Belgium[25] And when journalists on the ground can see with their own eyes that a military campaign is going horribly, chronically wrong, surely they have a wider responsibility to make this known. This is what happened when *The Times* revealed the disastrous state of the British army in the Crimean War in the 1850s and when American journalists exposed atrocities committed by their country's troops in Vietnam.

From the military perspective, however, media activity, enhanced by improvements in news media technology, is at best something to be managed to the maximum extent possible. The experience of television's power during the Vietnam War convinced political and military leaders that if you can keep journalists under strict control, you should do so. When Britain went to war with Argentina in 1982 over the latter's incursions into the Falkland Islands, the only way journalists could get to the war or transmit stories from it was with the aid of the Royal Navy. As a result, there was hardly any front-line reporting until the very final stages of the conflict. Even so, the British government complained vigorously when London-based journalists, especially those working for the BBC, insisted upon carrying reports from Argentinian sources.

By the time of a series of conflicts in the 1990s in the Gulf and the Balkans, military planners had to deal with the fact that media technology had moved on again. Now, television journalists could operate in the field with lightweight cameras which made it possible to shoot pictures and edit and transmit them from the field via satellite. The internet meant that when a radio station was bombed, or shut down (as was the case with the Belgrade station B92 in the Yugoslav wars), it could still reach listeners via the World Wide Web. By the late 1990s, news was happening around the clock on radio, television, and the internet. The days of a single, orderly news briefing a day, timed to serve the main evening news on television, was well and truly gone. In the Balkans, NATO quickly concluded that it would need to learn from the politicians of the Clinton and Blair era the techniques of spin, rapid rebuttal, and 'feeding the beast'—a technique designed to ensure that the 24-hour news media never suffer from the kind of hunger that encourages them to go looking for inconvenient stories and angles. 'Information' of dubious provenance about atrocities committed by the Serb armed forces on citizens of Kosovo were lent official support, only to be confirmed as false when the conflict ended and the 'information' about mass graves could be checked.

The Kosovo War of 1999 also spread literally to the World

Wide Web, when hackers from different factions tried to disrupt each others' web-based communications. The new openness of the communications system had other, startling effects. I recall sitting in a barber's shop in London during the early days of the allied bombardment of Belgrade and being taken aback to hear on a television phone-in the voices of people whose towns and cities allied aircraft were bombing. Meanwhile, the BBC News website, at the time the most visited news site in Europe, included direct hyperlinks to sites devoted to distributing information and propaganda on behalf of the Serb authorities, without apparent complaint from the authorities. As General Wesley Clark, supreme commander of NATO's forces during the war, commented: in future all wars would be fought on the assumption that the news media operate behind enemy lines.

Yet instant, continuous news also produced a perverse effect. With news everywhere, the public attention span seemed to shorten: even in time of war, correspondents' reports had to compete with features about improved diets and fashion. Faraway wars, which scarcely involved military casualties on the NATO side, could be mined for the most exciting bits, then forgotten as was the case when the dreary, routine bombing of northern Iraq continued year after year in the late 1990s and was barely reported in the Western media. The public was, no doubt,

Is that Winnie's ring you're wearing?

An extraordinary story in G2

Doctors – the new fertility gods

In G2. With today's television

OnLine

Toy stories

With all the best IT jobs

45p

NEWSPAPER OF THE YEAR

The Guardian

Massive air and missile strikes unleashed across defiant Yugoslavia

The onslaught begins

Newspaper of the Year award for the Guardian

2am news

First the dull thud, then the sky lit up with fire

On other pages

Law lords back Pinochet extradition

Record £93m package for boss of drugs firm

Inside

Page 5

Page 15

Page 21

7. When NATO launched air and missile strikes against Yugoslavia in March 1999, it was the first allied action on European soil since the end of the Second World War. But British newspapers didn't regard the event as a 'clear the front page' story: they felt that, even in a war, readers would still want a range of softer items, in the case of the *Guardian*, newspaper of the year, items on fertility treatment and romantic intrigue.

astonished to be told in 2002, as President George W. Bush talked up the idea of a decisive war against Iraq, that the First Gulf War had never, entirely, ended.

Editors were increasingly conscious that their readers, listeners, and viewers needed to be kept entertained and that hard news alone would no longer sell papers. This change was startlingly evident on the day when NATO bombers attacked Yugoslavia on 24 March 1999, the first NATO action on European soil since the end of the Second World War. The following day, only one British newspaper, the *Daily Telegraph*, thought the news justified clearing its front page for the event. The others all reported the news prominently, but felt they must offer other diversions for their readers. *The Times* obliged with a page 1 trail for a feature on the writer Bruce Chatwin's love affair with style-guru Jasper Conran. The *Guardian*'s preferred distraction was 'Doctors—the new fertility gods' and the *Independent*'s an item on England football managers.[26] In the week prior to the bombing, the proportion of each paper's space given to foreign news ranged between 8 and 12 per cent for the white broadsheets and between 0 and 4 per cent for the tabloids. Of the British newspapers, only the *Financial Times*, serving a globally minded business reader, has stood outside the trend of dramatically diminished weight of foreign news in the editorial mix.

The war in Afghanistan in 2001/2 raised different issues, involving a self-styled 'war against terrorism'. Faced with this threat, the British and American governments made explicit demands on their news media not to broadcast videotaped messages from the presumed terrorist leader, Osama bin Laden, on the grounds that these might contain coded messages to his supporters. This was widely regarded among journalists as very nearly as ludicrous as the action of the Thatcher government in the late 1980s in prohibiting broadcasters from transmitting the words of alleged Irish terrorists, with the result that viewers could see pictures of men like Gerry Adams, the leader of Sinn Fein, on television but had to rely upon subtitles for his words, unless they were lip readers. In practice, American TV news services did broadcast excerpts from the bin Laden tapes, whilst taking care not to offend the prevailing public mood.

The attacks on New York and Washington were quickly likened to the Japanese assault on Pearl Harbor, which drew the United States into the Second World War. In their coverage of the 'war against terror', news organizations vied with each other not only to be first with the news, but to declare their patriotism. Reporters wore patriotic badges in their lapels and NBC News's corporate symbol of the peacock acquired a stars and stripes embellishment. Fox News hired as its war correspondent a former talk-show host, Geraldo Rivera, who strutted in front of

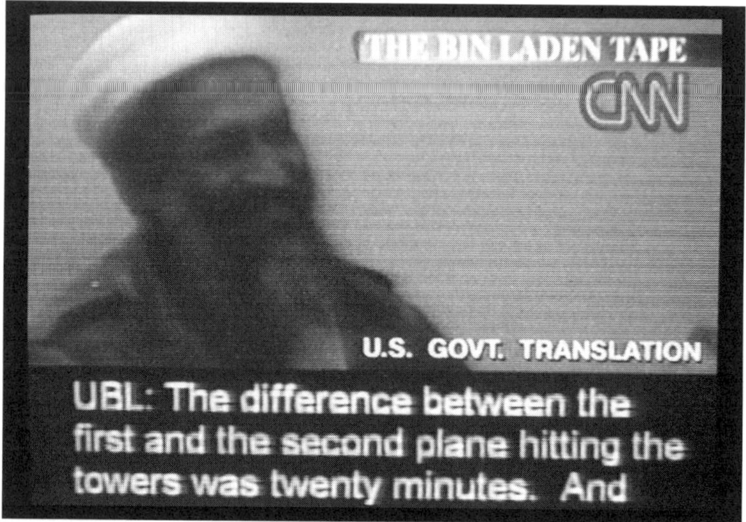

8. After the terrorist attacks on New York and Washington in September 2001, the Al Qaeda leader Osama bin Laden supplied videotaped messages via the Arabic television station Al Jazeera. The British and American governments put pressure on broadcasters not to broadcast the tapes, but most did so.

the camera, boasting of his willingness to shoot any passing Taliban fighter. With the *New York Times* devoting space for many weeks to an acclaimed series of stories about the victims of Ground Zero, some wondered aloud whether in such an atmosphere it was possible for even this illustrious newspaper to maintain a detached and critical eye on the course of American foreign policy.[27] Downie and Kaiser of the *Washington Post*, saw in the scale and seriousness of the American news media's reaction to this conflict both an accusation and a reason to hope. 'In the course of a few hours, the United States was transformed from a fat and happy enclave of peace and prosperity to a shaken victim of terrorist attacks. News organizations, from the best to the weakest, realised that all previous assumptions had been overtaken by events, at least for a time.' To the non-American ear, it did not sound probable that even an event as traumatic as this would shake American journalism out of a parochialism with such deep-rooted causes and such strikingly indicative symptoms as the fact that only one in five Americans has a passport. In the last thirty years, the average soundbite on American television news has fallen from 42 seconds to 8 seconds[28] and the proportion of time devoted to international news by US television networks has fallen from 45 to 13 per cent.[29] American newspapers are not much better, having cut the proportion of their editorial space devoted to foreign news from around 20 per cent to 2 per cent in the last two decades.[30]

Chris Cramer, the former BBC journalist who at the time of 11 September was president of CNN International Networks, tried explaining what was going on to readers of *Le Monde*. 'In America, the competition for viewers has done little to enlighten the audience about the outside world, with most of CNN's competitors focussing on US news only: local crime and baseball scores, today's weather forecast, this week's lottery winners and the latest fad of so-called reality television.'[31]

The Rise of Al Jazeera

A more significant outcome of the 'war on terror' was the emergence into public prominence of the Arab Al Jazeera television channel. Established in the mid-1990s as an Arabic-language television service by the BBC, but eventually ditched when the BBC's Saudi partner pulled out, Al Jazeera is financed by the emir of Qatar from a base in Doha and is believed to be the most watched television channel among 300 million Arabs living in twenty-two countries around the world.[32] Al Jazeera presents a rare challenge to the more or less complete global domination of English-language television news services, run by the likes of CNN, the BBC, Sky, and CNBC. It has, according to Nadim Shehadi of the Centre for Lebanese Studies in Oxford, also 'had an impact on the whole of the media in the region. The others are forced to catch up and compete—even the printed media. There's a lot more freedom now, because there's no point in controlling information if you know that people are going to find out from somewhere else.'[33]

By 2002, Al Jazeera had a staff of 350 journalists, including fifty foreign correspondents in thirty-one countries, serving an estimated audience of 35 million.[34] Its executives insist that it has imbibed its values of impartial reporting from the BBC, though its practice of describing Palestinian suicide bombers as 'martyrs' appears to many non-Arab observers to be an example of the violation of those standards. It operates out of a Gulf state, Qatar, whose unelected ruler funds Al Jazeera, and where 'public criticism of the ruling family or of Islam is forbidden'.[35] Yet it is also true that Al Jazeera has frequently found itself caught up in conflict with Arab governments, few of which can be described as democratically elected. Al Jazeera certainly prompted a large and worried response from the US Congress, which, following the 11/9 attacks, discussed a plan to spend $500m to create a rival Arab-language channel, designed to convey the American point of view. 'Al Jazeera changed the way Arabs watch TV as much as the September 11 attacks changed Americans,' say the authors of a book on the news service.[36]

The Other Big Brother

Al Jazeera, for sure, is one signpost towards the future. States may control, bully, or merely gently influence their national broadcasters, but increasingly audiences have the ability to choose their news suppliers, across international boundaries. 'Emphasis on the media's preponderant relationship with the state may overlook another important variable: the less easily traced flows of influence between media and audience,' says Susan Carruthers,[37] author of a study on the media, war, and terrorism. This does not mean that the nationally regulated, constrained broadcaster will disappear: if the political and public will exists, there is no reason at all why this should be so. But it does mean that such broadcasters will exist in a more competitive public sphere, with serious political implications for the politicians who determine the legal framework within which they work.

Optimists about the future of news believe that, in the end, the public will prefer quality, wide-ranging news services and be willing to pay for them. But even if that is true, it does not alter the fact that there is unprecedented competition in news and for the consumer's time generally. There was, on 11 September, something symbolic in the fact that a British tabloid newspaper, which like all its competitors in recent years had retreated from regular foreign news reporting, found itself scrambling to cover Ground Zero with the help of a sole correspondent, who had to drive 3,000 miles from his base in Los Angeles, where it is his routine task to cover Hollywood, not the rest of America.

The dangers in this state of affairs are obvious: that the easy affluence of Western societies turns out to be a narcotic, resulting in a false sense of security and a carelessness about problems not only on the other side of the world, but even those in the next neighbourhood, or lurking beneath the surface of everyday life. The 11 September suicide pilots' jets ploughed into the heart of a society that has often appeared to be more interested in stock markets and celebrities than politics and foreign affairs, in infotainment not information. In 1949, George Orwell warned of the dangers of a Big Brother state watching and controlling us. Half a century later, were we so busy watching 'reality TV' entertainment shows like *Big Brother* that we had become systematically blind to both the dangers and opportunities which surround us? Journalism's job is to find compelling ways to connect the public with these real realities and the democratic state's true long-term self-interest lies in the successful accomplishment of this mission.

3

Star-Struck

Journalism as Entertainment

IE STARR
ATE MY
HAMSTER

Freddie . . . "It's lies"

Journalism has always entertained as well as informed. Had it not done so, it would not have reached a mass audience. But today, say journalism's critics, the instinct to amuse is driving out the will, and depleting the resource, to report and analyse in any depth. Obsessed with a world of celebrity and trivia, the news media are rotting our brains and undermining our civic life.

There is no shortage of evidence. For Earth Day 2000, ABC News invited the handsome young actor and environmental campaigner, Leonardo DiCaprio, to conduct an interview with President Clinton for a prime-time network news show: a violation of journalistic values both on the grounds of DiCaprio's unfamiliarity with the art of rigorous interviewing and his partisanship on the subject, but justified by the network on the grounds of engaging a younger audience resistant to ageing authority figures like news anchors Tom Brokaw and Dan Rather. A related technique was used during the 1997 British general election when leading politicians, including the future Prime Minister Tony Blair, were interviewed for BBC television by stand-up comedians and other popular entertainers. Gordon

Brown, Britain's stern and lugubrious Chancellor of the Exchequer has been interviewed about British membership of the euro by a Scandinavian-born game-show hostess who subsequently enjoyed a further moment of fame when she conducted a brief and carefully publicized affair with the England football manager Sven Goran Eriksson at the time of the World Cup in 2002. Meanwhile, across the world, newspapers pile into the infotainment mêlée, competing to secure columns written in the name of the latest TV celebrity chef, gardener, or interior decorator. It is said that the highest paid writer in British newspapers is not a journalist at all, but the astrologist Jonathan Cainer, whose popular predictions have been placed at the service of circulation drives by a number of editors in recent years.

O. J. Simpson, Princess Diana, Britney Spears, Oprah Winfrey, and a procession of more ephemeral national sports stars are the names that mark the scenes of battle in the media's celebrity wars: all have made their impact upon newspapers and news broadcasters, boosting audiences, but contributing to a sense that the news business is losing its grip on reality, confusing popularity with significance, providing for readers and viewers what they appear to want, not what they really, really want or need. At its most successful, this celebrity system is even capable of inventing its own stars through specially concocted television events, which can then be exploited across all media platforms.

Thus, 'reality television' shows, like *Survivor*, *Big Brother*, and *Pop Idol*, generate new stars, who can be interviewed on the breakfast news shows and featured, day after day, on the pages of magazines and newspapers—and not just tabloid newspapers. Television station websites across North America and Europe attracted record traffic when they allowed viewers to vote on the fates of contestants in these games, which also can be followed, live, on 24-hour television channels or webcasts, even when all the participants in the event are sleeping. 'Nothing happening now, but something could at any moment, A lesson about how compartmentalised and safe so much television is now',[1] enthused Mark Thompson, the former BBC journalist shortly after he became chief executive of Channel 4 Television, owner of *Big Brother* rights in the UK. Even the terrors of global conflict sit in the spongy shadow of such fripperies. As the American satirical magazine and website, *The Onion*, put it in a spoof headline just a month after the 11 September attacks on Manhattan and Washington: 'Shattered Nation Longs to Care About Stupid Bullshit Again.'

To critics like Neil Postman, this is a prophecy triumphantly vindicated. Postman's 1985 book *Amusing Ourselves to Death*[2] made the case that television is, by its nature, a medium of entertainment, and that as it displaced print as the primary medium of news, it would result in a less-informed and less alert public: 'dumbing down' is the phrase that has come to signify this process. Television news, Postman says, with its music, drama, and glamorous personalities, 'is a format for entertainment, not for education, reflection or catharsis'.[3]

Yet this is no open-and-shut case. Television news is, especially in countries where it has been protected by strong regulation and benefited from massive public investment, regarded by most people not only as their main source of news but also their most trusted source. Might it be possible that today's proponents of 'tabloid tv' are merely following the path their tabloid newspaper forebears did: namely widening access to news and topical debate, and engaging with audiences who would otherwise be even less informed about, and engaged with, the events which shape their lives?[4]

The Tabloid Instinct

The tension between the news instinct and the entertainment instinct certainly isn't new. When William Randolph Hearst launched his *New York Mirror* in 1924 to take on America's first successful daily tabloid, the *New York Daily News*, he declared that the *Mirror* would provide '90 per cent entertainment, 10 per cent information—and the information without boring you'. If we are to understand so-called 'tabloid television', we need to consider the history of tabloid newspapers, which emerged to meet the demand of growing and literate urban populations in the late nineteenth century and which have constantly challenged the very definition of what journalism is, and the standards to be expected in its practice.

Strictly speaking, a tabloid is a newspaper page exactly half the size of a broadsheet page: a mathematical relationship which stems from the fact that publishers need to be able to print tabloid and broadsheet newspapers on the same printing presses. It is, in all sorts of ways, a misleading handle since the British tabloids which have given the term its contemporary meaning, the *Sun*, the *Daily Mail*, the *Daily Express*, and the *News of the World*, all began life as broadsheets and turned tabloid, respectively, in 1969, 1971, 1977, and 1984. It is also important to note that in many countries, the most respectable newspapers are tabloids, *Le Monde* and *El Pais* among them. So don't complain about 'tabloid journalism' in Paris or Madrid.

Modern tabloid journalism, although it has spread across Europe in titles like Germany's *Bild Zeitung*, is largely a product of transatlantic cross-pollination between Britain and the United States. It is worth sketching the history of British and American tabloid journalism, for it reveals the extent to which the values of entertainment and fact have often been indistinguishable.

In 1888, T. P. O'Connor, returned from the United States to

Britain to found an evening paper, *The Star*, giving us, in the words of Matthew Engel, historian of the British tabloid press, 'the frankest of all manifestos for the journalism that was to come'.[5] 'We believe,' O'Connor wrote:

> that the reader of the daily journal longs for other than mere politics; and we shall present him with plenty of entirely unpolitical literature—sometimes humorous, sometimes pathetic; anecdotal, statistical, the craze for fashions and the arts of housekeeping and, now and then, a short, dramatic and picturesque tale. In our reporting columns we shall do away with the hackneyed style of obsolete journalism; and the men and women that figure in the forum or the pulpit or the law court shall be presented as they are—living, breathing, in blushes or in tears—and not merely by the dead words that they utter.

After O'Connor successive waves of proprietors and editors would extend the dramatic licence of their writing, but they would often combine this with serious attempts at political influence. Northcliffe's *Daily Mail*, in the best tradition of popular journalism, beat a patriotic drum during the First World War, but also attacked Lord Kitchener, commander-in-chief of the British forces, for his incompetence in directing trench warfare. The Canadian Max Aitken, later Lord Beaverbrook, was famous for his circulation-building stunts, but he also promoted maverick political causes, prompting Prime Minister Stanley Baldwin to complain that newspaper publishers possess 'power without responsibility—the prerogative of the harlot throughout the ages'. The quality of Beaverbrook's own political judgement was evident in his complacent reaction to the rise of fascism in Germany. On 1 October 1938, the *Express*'s front page declared: YOU MAY SLEEP QUIETLY—IT IS PEACE FOR OUR TIME. Two days later, Hitler invaded Czechoslovakia.

The *Express*'s political misjudgements, along with its failure to read the changing aspirations and tastes of the working class, created space for the *Daily Mirror*, which had begun life in 1903 as a paper aimed at women, before pioneering in the 1920s the use of pictures. The *Mirror* read the situation in Germany more accurately (SOME DAY SOMEONE WILL HAVE TO STOP HITLER: IT MAY BE US) and after the war quickly became the biggest selling paper in the country.

Silvester Bolam, the *Mirror*'s editor from 1948 to 1953, felt no need to apologize for a louder, brasher style of journalism, announcing on his first front page: 'The *Mirror* is a sensational newspaper. We make no apology for that. We believe in the sensational presentation of news and views, especially important news and views, as a necessary and valuable service in these days of mass readership and democratic responsibility.' Sensationalism, Bolam said on a later occasion, 'does not mean distorting the truth. It means the vivid and dramatic presentation of events so as to give them a forceful impact on the mind of the reader. It means big headlines, vigorous writing, simplification into familiar, everyday language, and wide use of illustration by cartoons and photographs.' By 1967, under the leadership of Hugh Cudlipp, the *Mirror* was selling 5.3 million copies a day, in a country with a population of 50 million.

Murdoch Goes Further

But by the late 1960s, the Mirror had a competitor snapping at its heels. The *Sun* first appeared in 1964, as a renamed *Daily Herald*, a paper supported by and loyal to Britain's trade unions, but it was in deep trouble by 1969 when it was bought by Rupert Murdoch, the young Australian newspaper owner who had already purchased the *News of the World*, the naughtiest and best-selling of Britain's Sunday newspapers. The *News of the World*'s circulation had peaked in 1950 at an astonishing 8.5 million and went on to set a number of records, including the unprecedently high payment of £23,000 it made for the memoirs of Christine Keeler, the society prostitute whose revelations led to the resignation of John Profumo, the war minister, in 1963.

Murdoch told staff that he wanted the *Sun* to focus upon 'sex, sport and contests', a mission translated in the satirical paper *Private Eye* as 'a tearaway paper with a lot of tit'. *Private Eye* labelled Murdoch 'the Dirty Digger', well before the paper's

NEWS OF THE WORLD

EMPIRE NEWS

Confessions of Christine

BY THE GIRL WHO IS ROCKING THE GOVERNMENT

TODAY the News of the World starts publishing the full confessions of 21-year-old Christine Keeler, the girl who has rocked the Government, the model whose life in high and not-so-high society has set the world talking.

On Pages Four and Five will be found the first real and authentic account of the startling events which culminated in the resignation of Mr. John Profumo, the War Minister.

Arrested yesterday

Premier will face Tory critics

New TV strike threat

HOW MUCH IS IT WORTH TO SAVE YOUR HAIR?

Billy Cotton collapses

GUNMAN WOUNDS 3

9. At the time, the £23,000 paid by the *News of the World* for the 'confessions' of society prostitute Christine Keeler in 1963 was the heftiest piece of 'cheque-book journalism' in history. Today, newspapers routinely pay for stories.

launch in 1970 of a regular feature, which continues to this day: a photograph of a naked young women on page three. As recently as October 2002, the *Sun* was publicly congratulating itself on the emergence of a *Sun*-lookalike in Moscow (dubbed, inevitably, the *Sun-ski)* complete with Page Three 'lovelies.' The *Sun*'s

Page Three Girl has also made a successful move to the paper's website, where she must feel rather prim, compared with some of the other things going on around her on the World Wide Web.

By the time the *Sun* soared past the *Mirror* in 1977, Murdoch was buying newspapers in the United States, first in Texas, then, in 1976, the *New York Post*. In Britain, faced with a challenge from the newly launched *Daily Star*, Murdoch brought in a new editor, Kelvin Mackenzie, who combined an ability to stretch the limits of taste and professional behaviour, with a passionate advocacy for the newly elected Margaret Thatcher, whose backing Murdoch would need as he developed his television ambitions in the UK. With Murdoch's business interests now spanning the Atlantic and Pacific Oceans, cross-fertilization between Australian, British, and American tabloid journalism intensified.

By the time of Margaret Thatcher's war against Argentina in 1982, which generated Mackenzie's famous headline GOTCHA, when the Argentinian warship *General Belgrano* was torpedoed by a British submarine, Mackenzie was into his stride. The paper sometimes brilliantly caught the mood of the frustrated, but aspirational working-class people who supported Thatcher, but it also thumbed its nose at standards. During the Falklands War, the *Sun* published an 'interview' with the widow of a dead serviceman with whom the paper had never spoken. Seven years later, under a front-page headline, THE TRUTH, the paper accused Liverpool football fans of urinating upon rescue workers as they tried to save people in a stadium disaster in which ninety-six fans were crushed to death. This and other *Sun* angles on the Hillsborough story was never substantiated, resulting in damage to the paper's sales on Merseyside from which it has never recovered. In his final period as editor, Mackenzie also became careless with the libel laws, costing his boss a fortune in payments to stars like Elton John.

Sometimes, Mackenzie's front pages would disappear entirely into a world of make-believe. There is no other explanation for headlines like the famous FREDDIE STARR ATE MY HAMSTER, on 13 March 1986, referring to an obscure incident two years earlier, when Starr, a comedian, had pretended to eat a hamster in a sandwich as a joke. On many days, it became impossible to tell the difference between the *Sun*'s reports of death or adultery in the street of a popular television soap opera and similar dramas in real life. The paper had turned fact into fiction and fiction into fact, which amused readers but not the real-life individuals who found themselves caught up in the *Sun* soap opera. In the 1990s, the *Sun*'s star columnist, Richard Littlejohn, would habitually conclude one of his ranting columns with the exasperated catchphrase: 'you couldn't make it up.' But you could and the *Sun* sometimes has.

THE Sun

£50,000 BINGO Lucky numbers are on Page 18

Thursday, March 13, 1986 18p TODAY'S TV IS ON PAGE 14

FREDDIE STARR ATE MY HAMSTER

Comic put a live pet in sandwich, says beauty

EXCLUSIVE by DICK SAXTY

ZANY comic Freddie Starr put a live hamster in a sandwich and ATE it, model girl Lea La Salle claimed yesterday.

BITE

JEWEL IN MY CROWN

Vicar praises rape daughter

Justice

SELLERS GIRL IS CHARGED IN DRUG CASE Page 5

10. Freddie Starr ate my Hamster. Oh no he didn't. Tabloid newspapers frequently invent stories for the entertainment of their readers, or run with what might charitably be described as fanciful headlines. This classic, in the *Sun*, related vaguely to a stunt two years previously in which Starr, a comedian, pretended to eat a hamster.

Mackenzie's *Sun*, however, has to be understood in the context of the tabloid story in the United States. America's first successful daily tabloid, the *New York Daily News*, had appeared in 1919 and prompted one of the great newspaper wars of the century, when William Randoph Hearst launched the *New York Mirror* against it. But it was a Hearst broadsheet, the *New York Enquirer*, which was to change the course of tabloid history when it was picked up, with a circulation of 17,000, by Generoso Pope Jr in 1952.

The Pope of American Tabloids

Pope, who knew and admired the *News of the World*, renamed the paper the *National Enquirer*, turned it tabloid and told his small team of journalists to concentrate upon lurid crime stories. Fifteen years later, having acquired a slew of competitors, the *Enquirer* was selling a million copies a week. By 1975, by pioneering the technique of selling at the supermarket check-out, the *Enquirer*'s circulation hit five million, attracting another competitor in Rupert Murdoch's newly launched *Star*. In 1978, an edition of the *Enquirer* featuring a photograph of the body of Elvis Presley sold seven million copies, a peak not since exceeded. Behind this circulation graph, remarkable in a country which in the 1970s had no truly nationwide daily newspapers, is one of journalism's more extraordinary stories.

Generoso Pope pioneered a garish style of journalism which, like Mackenzie's, had moments of high political impact. It was the *Enquirer*'s photograph in 1988 of presidential candidate Gary

Hart on board a yacht called *Monkey Business*, with a young woman called Donna Rice on his lap, that ended his political career. Although there is a debate to be had about the press's appetite for the private lives of public figures, this story could not be challenged, since Hart was indeed concealing an illicit relationship.

But countless other tabloid stories were simply made up. At one edge of the *Enquirer*'s market, tabloids with innocuous titles like *News Extra* and *Midnight* specialized in bizarre headlines, supported by alluring narratives and doctored photographs, usually dreamt up during boozed-up editorial conferences in bars. The inspiration of these publications was closer to that of satirical comics like *National Lampoon* or *The Onion*, which are manifest self-parodies of journalism and its techniques, though it is not certain that all of their readers viewed them in these terms. Presumably, only the most die-hard conspiracy theorists would have believed a headline like HITLER SEEN ALIVE IN US or JFK ALIVE ON SKORPIOS (complete with picture) and it is difficult to think that anyone took seriously: SEVEN-HOUR ENEMA TURNS BLACK GIRL WHITE! But what were they to make of MOM CLEANS KIDS BY PUTTING THEM IN CLOTHES WASHER? Or, GIRL, 16, BECOMES A GRANDMOTHER, not to mention I CUT OUT HER HEART AND STOMPED ON IT or I WAS RAPED EIGHT DAYS BY THREE MEN AND A LESBIAN. The closer tabloid invention interplayed with news of the real world, the greater its impact.

Bill Sloan, who worked on the *National Enquirer* and other tabloids, has explained how experienced writers and editors like himself 'were routinely able to shift gears between out-and-out trash and serious reportage. One day they were inventing bogus stories for *News Extra* or even grinding out soft-core porn for the *National Bulletin*. . . . The next day, they were interviewing real people, writing legitimate articles, and striving mightily for documentation and credibility.'[6] Sloan's justification for this behaviour, apart from the excellent salaries which attracted numerous émigrés from Britain and Australia to 'Tabloid Valley' in Florida, to where the *Enquirer* had been moved, was that

> these journalists had rediscovered a basic truth about their profession. They recognized early on what William Randolph Hearst had figured out eighty years earlier and what practically every TV news executive and major-daily editor realizes today—what qualifies as hot news has only the sketchiest relationship to pure information. For all their lofty pretences, today's mainstream media are essentially just another branch of show biz.

Faking It

Sloan's logical explanation for the decline of tabloid circulations in the 1980s and 1990s is that all newspapers, along with most television, had to some degree or another adopted a similar viewpoint, so that the broadsheets were out-tabloiding the tabloids. British broadsheet newspapers, for example, in recent years have run numerous fictional columns, mostly with comic or satirical purpose, but occasionally misjudging the ability of their readers to recognize what is a joke. One such effort had the writer, unknown to the reader a well-known television satirist, pledging to commit suicide. The same satirist, Chris Morris, used his television show to lure celebrities into invented schemes and situations designed to show them in a bad light. Apologists for this genre of television sometimes call it 'investigative comedy'.

Things did not look so funny, however, when some high-profile examples of conventional journalism also turned out to be invented. In 1996, a British documentary team working for Carlton Television faked sequences in a story about drug-running in South America, for which the company was fined £2m by the television industry regulator, a form and scale of punishment impossible in the unregulated press. Shortly afterwards, it emerged that even the venerable BBC was using actors to pose as real people with real problems, on a daily talk show hosted by Vanessa Feltz. In 1981, a young *Washington Post* reporter called Janet Cooke was stripped of her Pulitzer Prize when it turned out that her award-winning story of child drug addiction was a concoction. Another newspaper columnist pretended to be suffering from cancer in order to make her column more appealing to readers.

Celebrities Squared

In the same period that journalism has learnt to make light of the boundary between fact and fiction, it has also become increasingly absorbed by the entertainment and sales potential of celebrity, with significant consequences for the way that journalism is practised.

One especially damaging consequence is that, in order to get pictures and stories about celebrities, journalists have to deal with the industry of agents, publicists, and middle people which surrounds them and who make their own living from promoting the celebrity's brand values through obtaining the 'right' media coverage. This is a strictly two-way commercial play, because the news media know that the right celebrity cover on a magazine, or star interview on a talk show, can boost sales and ratings in a way nothing else does for the same price. Celebrity is thus big money not only for the celebrities, but also for the news media. It is inevitable that, in these circumstances, stories and pictures will be obtained not, chiefly, by the industry and enterprise of reporters, but by those news media willing to pay the largest fees and guarantee the most favourable treatment for the star in question.

Generoso Pope discovered the power of celebrity when, in 1969, the *National Enquirer* published a family photograph of the late President Kennedy, surrounded by a story headlined: JACKIE BLASTED BY NURSE WHO BROUGHT UP JFK'S CHILDREN.[7] Sales of the *Enquirer* increased by almost a third, prompting Pope to dispatch the following instruction to his staff: 'I want her on the cover at least every couple of weeks.' This they did, often embellishing pictures with stories of the purest fiction, claiming Mrs Onassis had changed religion, allowed her children to grow marijuana at home, and turned her second husband's hair white.

Much the same phenomenon attended the tragic figure of Diana, Princess of Wales, who entered global media consciousness in September 1980 when she was identified as the likely bride of Prince Charles, heir to the British throne. During the fairy-tale phase of the royal romance, the princess appeared on page one of the *Sun* sixteen times in a single month. When she chose to go on the BBC Television current affairs programme *Panorama*, in 1995, to discuss the breakdown of her marriage, the programme had the biggest audience in its history. No wonder the press was willing to pay huge sums for any snatched, or even doctored picture of Diana, and that so many were on her tail as she sped, driven by a drunk, into a Parisian underpass in August 1997.

At her funeral, the princess's brother famously accused the press of having his sister's 'blood on their hands' for the manner in which they had hounded her. On the other side of the Atlantic, the *National Enquirer* was quickly trying to recall and pulp its latest edition which led with the startling headline: DI GOES SEX MAD: 'I CAN'T GET ENOUGH!' Disgusted by press behaviour towards the princess, other celebrities, including Madonna, George Clooney, Elizabeth Taylor, Tom Cruise, and Sylvester Stallone, called for stronger counter-attacks in the courts on the tabloids. But the trouble with the Diana affair, like so many other celebrity outrages, was that it was a two-way, not a one-way street. In the late 1980s the *Sunday Times* was accused of printing unsubstantiated lies about the troubled Charles and Diana relationship, based upon its expensive purchase of serialization rights to a book by Andrew Morton, but it turned out that Diana had been the primary source of Morton's information, handing instructions through an intermediary. Long after Diana's death, the ironies surrounding news media coverage of the British royal family continued to compound themselves. In 2002, a television team was spotted breaking a general

THE EXPRESS ON SUNDAY

AUGUST 31, 1997 — 75p

DIANA IS DEAD

6AM NEWS SPECIAL

Princess and Dodi killed in car smash

BY JACK GEE in Paris and JAMES EADIE in London

PRINCESS Diana died last night after being injured in a car chase in a Paris tunnel.

She suffered a fatal heart attack in hospital where she was being treated for serious injuries after being cut free from the wreckage of her mangled Mercedes.

The attack was brought on by a massive lung haemorrhage. Doctors had fought for two hours to save her.

Her boyfriend Dodi Fayed died at the crash scene, close to the River Seine.

The couple were being pursued by paparazzi at speeds of up to 100 mph when their car careered into the central reservation of a tunnel, before rolling over several times and smashing into the tunnel wall.

After hours of fevered speculation about the gravity of the Princess' injuries, the tragic news was confirmed doctors at the hospital.

Her death was announced outside the hospital by French Interior Minister Jean-Pierre Chevenement and later confirmed by Buckingham Palace.

Prince Charles was informed immediately at Balmoral where he broke the news to Princes William and Harry. Dodi's father, Mohamed Al Fayed flew to Paris as soon as news of the accident broke. The 36-year-old

PAGE 3 COLUMN 6

CRASH SCENE: The wreckage of Diana's and Dodi's car in the tunnel under the Seine after the 100mph crash

WORLD NEWS 29-31 • OPINION 36 • CROSSWORD 68 • MONEY 73-80 • TV 91-96 • WEATHER 94

11. After her marriage to Prince Charles, heir to the British throne, Princess Diana quickly became one of the few celebrity faces guaranteed to push up newspaper and magazine circulations in markets all around the world. When she died in a Parisian road tunnel, pursued by press photographers, in August 1997, tabloid newspapers came under attack. At her funeral, the Princess's brother accused publishers of having 'blood on their hands'.

agreement to avoid harassing Charles and Diana's son Prince William at university. It turned out that the crew belonged to the TV production company owned by Charles's younger brother, Prince Edward.

Warhol and the News Hole

Perhaps we should recall that the very word 'paparazzi' has its origin not in fact but fiction. Signore Paparazzo is the pushy photographer in Federico Fellini's 1960 film, *La Dolce Vita*, foreshadowing the point that in the last decades of the twentieth century, faction and fiction bled into each on every front. Andy Warhol, the iconic artist of the pop generation, took routine news agency snaps of car crashes, including some considered by newspapers too gory for publication, and retouched them into art. And among his most admired works are the images of celebrities, often repeated, frame after irresistible frame.

Today, celebrity publishing is a free-standing industry. *Hello Magazine* began its life in Spain as *¡Hola!*, identifying a much copied niche for soft, mainly photographic profiles based upon handsome payments and access to the star's private world, including weddings, funerals, new babies, and homes. One of *Hello*'s imitators, the UK magazine *OK*, is owned by Richard Desmond, whose other properties include pornographic magazines and television channels, as well as the *Daily Express*. When

Desmond bought the newspaper group, he immediately set out to exploit *OK*'s celebrity contracts, including the magazine's relationship with David and Victoria Beckham, at the time Britain's most pursued celebrity couple, across his new titles. At the same time, the Beckhams were busily extending their own brand, by advertising sun-glasses, potato crisps, and other fast-moving consumer goods. The fact that celebrities would take part in flattering magazine features one week, then denounce tabloids the next for intrusion into their personal lives, has tended to undermine their arguments in the courts for greater privacy, as the 'supermodel' Naomi Campbell found when she lost a legal action in 2002 against the *Daily Mirror*, which had revealed her recourse to treatment for drug addiction. The newspapers could ask: why should stars be licensed to manipulate their relationship with the fans whose cash makes them rich?

For the individual journalist, the celebrity boom raises another, more routine difficulty, in that celebrities, like any other individual in heavy demand, tend to be able to dictate the terms on which they do business with the news media. The result is that, when journalists are granted interviews with celebrities, they frequently agree to notify questions in advance and even to submit their copy for vetting prior to publication, not to mention often being obliged to pay cash for the access in the first place. Interviewees also sometimes demand inclusion of references to commercial sponsors. There is a pleasant parody of the routine (five-minute) celebrity interview in the film *Notting Hill*, in which Hugh Grant poses as a journalist from *Horse and Hound* magazine to interview Julia Roberts. It is a situation which makes the manipulations of the Westminster political lobby or the White House press corps look positively low-key. As Caroline Monnot of *Le Monde* protested during the French presidential election campaign in 2002, even the ultra-left candidate of Lutte Ouvriere was seen 'borrowing the tactics from movie stars' agents. Accreditations have to be applied for, there are waiting lists and you only get three timed questions with the star. It's as though you were interviewing Julia Roberts.'[8] Just so.

Journalists as Celebs

In this climate, perhaps we should not be surprised that journalists too, especially television journalists, have themselves turned into celebrities.

Barbara Walters has gone down in history as the first million dollar news presenter—her annual reward for co-presenting ABC's nightly news in the mid-1970s. This was in the era when Van Gordon Sauter, head of CBS News, propounded an influential theory that, since journalism was 'a kind of theatre', what he wanted to see from his correspondents and producers were 'moments' rather than facts. Such moments, he said, offered 'a portrait of an emotional reality'.[9] Since then, the salaries of news presenters have multiplied tenfold and, like sports stars, actors and models, some appear to be heavily concerned with maximizing the value of their brand, whether on the lecture circuit, opening supermarkets, hosting executive conferences, or even associating themselves with product sponsorship.

News executives account for these developments and defend them by saying that the public is attracted by celebrities. If stars are what you need to get ordinary people to pay attention to news, and so to become better informed, this is a legitimate technique, no different in principle from the skilful use of pictures in magazines or headlines in newspapers. There is no doubt, however, that the rise of the celebrity presenter and correspondent has been accompanied, certainly in the case of the US television networks, by a decimation of their overseas reporting resources. Media companies know that a handful of celebrities may look expensive, but they are nowhere near as expensive as extensive reporting networks. And in any case, why keep a well-informed but unglamorous foreign reporter in London, New York, Rome, or Tokyo, when if there's a big story, the audience 'wants to see' the star roving correspondent or anchor, live from the news scene?

There are, however, striking ill-effects. First of all, fly-in, fly-away presenters are no subsitute for reporters who know the terrain and who can make judgements based upon much off-air inquiry. Stars are seldom in a place long enough to find anything out. These days, it is not at all unusual for an on-the-spot reporter to be given the latest news he is supposed to be 'reporting' on the phone or by email from head office, in order to then appear before the camera and pretend that he or she has just discovered it on the spot. News stars can also have the effect of overshadowing the events they have gone to report, so the audience finds itself more concerned with the latest hairstyle or dress of the celebrity than with the sometimes harrowing reality upon which they are reporting. Many journalists would add to this list the evident danger that, in a world where presentational values replaces values of substance, television news will always be inclined to hire people who look glamorous, rather than those who can ask the sharpest questions and assess the news situation with greatest authority. Some such comments doubtless reflect the frustration felt by any generation of human beings as they are forced to make space for their juniors. But there is a reason why the *Washington Post*'s desk-book or guidelines on 'the reporter's role' reads: 'Although it has become increasingly difficult for this newspaper and for the press generally to do so since Watergate, reporters should make every effort to remain in the audience, to be the stagehand rather than the star, to report the news, not to make the news.'[10]

There are also, it should be said, many exceptions to the characterization of the television presenter as lead air-head in a theatre of pretence. John Simpson, the BBC's veteran world affairs editor, spends most of his life on the road and is a formidable expert in international affairs, as well as being a gifted writer and broadcaster. The fact that even he got caught up in a ludicrous characterization as the 'liberator of Kabul', when the Afghan capital fell to American and British backed Northern Alliance forces in 2001, demonstrated that even the oldest and most practised hands occasionally lose their grip and forget that great television journalism is all about teamwork.

The Afghan War provided a stage for a newer breed of star correspondent, Geraldo Rivera, who was hired to cover the conflict by Fox News, the American all-news channel launched by Rupert Murdoch's News Corporation in 1996. Rivera, a moustachioed one-time talk-show host, dubbed by the *New York Times*, 'the face of trash TV',[11] strutted in front of the camera, whispering emotionally about the 'hallowed ground' where American servicemen were said, wrongly it turned out, to have died. 'He has turned the war zone into a vast shrine to himself,' lamented the *Wall Street Journal*.[12]

Richard Sambrook, director of BBC News, says the corporate pressures are constantly intensifying to focus upon celebrity reporters and presenters and to downgrade the emphasis upon news-gathering. American networks increasingly pool their news pictures, in order to save money, because they regard their critical brand difference as revolving around their on-camera stars. 'On-screen talent, not content, is becoming the basis of difference between rival American news broadcasters and we are starting to see those same pressures in Britain,' says Sambrook.[13]

None of this is to suggest that it is easy to disentangle the claims of entertainment from the claims of news and good journalism. The most effective journalism achieves both. But it is clear that money can distort the picture in very many ways. As Don Hewitt, the creator of the CBS current affairs show *60 Minutes*, which is the benchmark for high-rating current affairs television in the US, has said: 'We want the companies we work for to put back the wall the pioneers erected to separate news from entertainment, but we are not above climbing over the rubble each week to take an entertainment-size pay cheque for broadcasting news.'[14]

In Defence of Tabloids

What then of the case for the defence for tabloid journalism? Curiously, this comes these days more loudly from outside the news industry than from within it. The starting point is that much criticism of tabloid journalism is, as Silvester Bolam understood, little more than snobbery: the disdainful view of the man and woman in the best seats at the opera for the couple who prefer watching soap opera on television. 'The *Sun* stands for opportunities for working people and for change in this society. It's a real catalyst for change, it's a very radical paper,' Rupert Murdoch once said[15] and there have been periods when this claim has been justified, whatever you think about Page Three Girls or Kelvin Mackenzie's way with facts. There is no escaping the fact that the old establishments, especially in politics, which live or die by popular support, not only need the support of tabloid readers, they need to be able to speak in language to which those readers will respond, if democracy and public life are to thrive.

An illustration of this point emerged in the mid-1990s during the exhaustive media coverage of the trial of O. J. Simpson, the black footballer accused of murdering his wife and a male friend, and which has been linked with the growing reluctance of black Americans to serve on juries or, when they do, to behave in the manner expected by the court. After the Simpson trial, Dan Lungren, California's attorney general, complained about the 'oprahisation' of American juries—a reference to the heated debates, leading to instant judgement, which takes place on television talk shows like the one hosted by Oprah Winfrey. 'Talk show watchers are widely considered by prosecutors and professional jury consultants to be more likely than

12. Oprah Winfrey, the American talk-show host, has become a legendary figure in what some people call 'tabloid television', typically broadcast in the daytime and featuring live, studio based discussions with strong audience participation. According to critics, the 'oprah-ization' of American culture has involved diminished respect for authority, obsession with personal dramas, and 'dumbed down' television. Oprah's supporters say she has been a key figure in democratizing American public life, giving a voice to people usually ignored by the media.

others to distrust official accounts of "the truth",'[16] Lungren said.

Regrettable though this tendency, if true, may be from the point of view of an attorney general, it must be balanced against the possibility that trustworthiness of 'official accounts of truth' might indeed be legitimately doubted by black people. In the words of Kevin Glynn, an academic commentator, tabloid media

> multiplies and amplifies the heterogenous voices and viewpoints in circulation in contemporary culture, giving rein to many that are typically excluded from the dominant regime of truth through the

dynamics of race, class, gender, age and sexuality. The shrill and revulsive response to tabloid media from 'respectable' journalism and other elite social quarters indicates the extent to which their popularity threatens officialdom's power to regulate the discursive procedures through which we make sense of society and ourselves. 'Serious' journalism is far more concerned with controlling, organizing, and ordering the hierarchy of voices it admits into its discursive reportoir than is tabloid news, whose contents are driven by ratings and circulation.'[17]

Which is exactly what Rupert Murdoch was saying, in plainer language.

Catharine Lumby, an Australian journalist and academic, has gone further, arguing that talk shows like Winfrey's 'exemplify a new form of public speech, one which privileges experience over knowledge, emotion over reason, and popular opinion over expert advice'.[18] 'Western public spheres have become a forum for voices and interests which were largely excluded from public debate even thirty years ago.' She could have added that among the consequences of Winfrey's style, and her celebrity, was the development of the most successful book club in American literary history, as the television star's book club show in the late 1990s became for a period the key driver of the country's best-seller lists.[19]

Jesse 'the Body' Ventura

Glynn brings to his advocacy for tabloid journalism a specifically political case, involving the election to the governorship of Minnesota in 1998 of Jesse 'the Body' Ventura, a former professional wrestler and radio talk-show 'shock jock'. Glynn sees the very high turnout in this election (over 60 per cent, compared with less than 50 per cent even for presidential races) resulting from Ventura's fluency with tabloid-style communication, that enabled him to assemble an extraordinary coalition of supporters, many of them normally excluded from the political domain. This is a counter-argument to the mainstream debate about dumbing down which deserves a serious hearing. As David Kamp suggested in an influential article in *Vanity Fair*: 'the tabloidification of American life—of the news, of the culture, yea, of human behaviour—is such a sweeping phenomenon that it can't be dismissed as merely a jokey footnote to the history of the 1990s. Rather, it's the very hallmark of our times; if the decade must have a name . . . it might as well be the Tabloid Decade.'[20]

This is the cultural context in which newspaper and television executives find themselves working when they try to make their political coverage more directly relevant to readers and viewers, looking for 'news you can use' rather than news which fits into a hazy consensus of the news canon. It is a difficult line to tread between appealing to the audience's natural point of interest and emotional pressure points, without trivializing events. It cannot be denied that there is plenty of bad tabloid journalism which leads its consumers into escapism and ignorance or which, worse still, bullies its victims and deepens prejudices, often among the most vulnerable groups such as asylum seekers. But there is also brilliant tabloid journalism, in newspapers, magazines, television, and radio, that brings issues alive and broadens popular engagement. Those who worry that that once serious newspapers like the *New York Times*, the *Guardian*, or *La Repubblica* have diminished themselves by including, alongside news and analysis about politics and world events, features about restaurants and personal hygiene, should probably relax. Today's broadsheet newspaper reader is also a child of the Tabloid Decade, which declares it permissible to be interested in football and Wagner or the United Nations and *Big Brother*. What matters is whether people, faced with an apparently vast choice of sources of news and other topical information, know where and how to find the information they need and that, one way or another, they are able to operate as informed citizens.

Conducting focus groups with a very wide range of people in 2002, for a research project aimed at understanding the way people get news and how well they are served by it, I was struck again and again by the genuine hunger of people to understand issues, like the risks of certain vaccination programmes for their children, or the real patterns of crime in their neighbourhood, and that too often they feel that no one is providing the information, or making it accessible to them.

But as people have come to rely more and more on television news, they have come up against two problems. The first is that television news is free at the point of consumption and, essentially, ambient in the sense that today you have to make an effort to avoid it, rather than collide with it. Nor with television, radio, and the internet must you pay directly to get news and even many newspapers today are given away as advertising-supported 'free sheets'. We found that young people, unlike their elders, identify quite strongly with the statement that news is something which you follow when you are already aware something interesting is going on: a rational response in an era of ambient news. The second problem is that very little television news is truly local, which means that people feel decreasingly confident in their knowledge about what is going on in their own neighbourhoods.[21] For many people in Britain today it is easier to find out what is going on in the Indian subcontinent or American baseball than on the next street.

In the end, these concerns are of greater importance than the debate about the tabloidization of news. News has always been conveyed in a wide range of styles, and with a wide range of content. We only have a problem with tabloidization if it drives out other types of journalism and diminishes diversity. The greater danger to diversity, however, may arise from changes in the ownership of the news media.

4

Up to a Point

Lord Copper's: Who owns Journalists

Journalists regard themselves, and are regarded by others, as free-spirited individuals; mavericks not easily bound by corporate rule and regulation or, in certain situations, even by the law of the land. Yet almost all modern journalism takes place within a corporate setting, which limits and influences what journalists do. True, the internet, with its list-publishing and web-log technology ('blogging') has again made it possible for journalists who lack access to a mainstream media outlet to publish their own work, so long as they are not too concerned about financial rewards, but most journalists work for someone and usually for an organization. That someone might be a press baron of the kind the American commentator A. J. Liebling had in mind when he remarked that freedom of the press exists only for those who happen to own one. Which is why the internet, with its self-publishing possibilities, has been referred to as 'Liebling's revenge'. The question is: what effect do different forms of ownership have upon journalism?

It is important to clear up one misunderstanding from the start. These days, the news media are for the most part not run by press barons. The story of contemporary journalism is of the slackening grip of the cigar-chomping tyrant who barks out orders for editorial lines, while devising promotional campaigns and plotting the demise of some nearby president or prime minister. The baron's origins lie in the multifunctional owners of small printing shops in the pre-industrial era, when publishers literally wrote, printed, distributed, and sold the advertisements for their newspapers. Today, we are rather shocked when an anachronistic figure like the Canadian Lord Conrad Black, owner of the *Daily Telegraph* and the *Jerusalem Post*, writes in one of his own titles. By the late 1980s, when the outsize baronial figure, Czech-born Robert Maxwell owned the *Daily Mirror*, it was considered very exotic that he wished to see his own photograph on the paper's own front page, though he made it to everyone's front page when he robbed the *Mirror* pension scheme and vanished into the sea off Tenerife from the back of his baronial yacht in November 1991.

Corporate Man Cometh

Today's typical news media boss is not a Maxwell, Black, or Rupert Murdoch. The modern boss does not have ink or even necessarily entrepeneurship in his veins. He is most likely a professional manager, working in a corporate setting, and increasingly that corporate setting will entail involvement in a wide range of media, from the internet to movies, spread across many parts of the world. At the time of writing, AOL–Time Warner is the largest and most conspicuous of these multimedia beasts, being a fusion of the old Time Inc, Warner Brothers' film and music interests, and America Online, a pioneer of the commercial internet. AOL–Time Warner also owns several other large businesses, including Britain's IPC magazine group and CNN, the global television news service. In the same period that this empire was being assembled, Walt Disney snapped up ABC and Viacom bought CBS, though before long Disney was in talks with AOL about a possible combination of CNN and ABC.

It is necessary to stress 'at the time of writing' since ownership of news media is, like anything governed by financial markets, notoriously unstable, and most business mergers fail to achieve their intended advantages. There is no certainty that the current fashion for companies to build pan-media businesses will meet with success in business terms. Only a couple of decades ago an entirely opposing fashion held sway. Then, diverse industrial conglomerates thought it was a good idea to own a few media assets, sometimes as an intellectual diversion for their owners or senior executives, but also because this was a period when the stock market admired diverse asset bases, supposedly capable of evening out performance over the ups and downs of economic cycles. This was the era which made NBC part of General Electric and CBS a sister company of Westinghouse. At that time Pearson, one of Britain's few players in the global media business, combined interests ranging from investment banking and crockery to theme parks, alongside the *Financial Times*, Penguin Books, and Australia's Grundy Television, producer of the soap opera *Neighbours*. Today, we have returned to a period when management textbooks enthuse over companies which 'stick to their knitting'.

In global media terms, American companies are dominant simply because their domestic market is so much larger than any other and their language widely spoken. They occupy roughly thirty slots in the list of the world's fifty largest media companies. The big non-American players include Germany's Bertelsmann, France's Vivendi, and Japan's Sony. The last is an interesting example of a company which began in electrical equipment and diversified into content, buying into Hollywood and recorded music.

When Press Barons Ruled the Earth

But the image of the hiring, firing, government-toppling press baron dies hard. He (and it nearly always was a he—Katharine Graham, who inherited the *Washington Post* and led it during the Watergate investigation is a notable exception) was in his prime in North America and Europe in the period from the last years of the nineteenth century to the 1930s. This was the era of

Joseph Pulitzer and W. Randolph Hearst in the United States, the latter satirized but also immortalized in the semi-fictional persona of Citizen Kane, the brooding genius who constructed a newspaper empire that shook American society, before retreating to the garrisoned privacy of San Simeon, the Pacific Coast retreat which came to be known as Hearst Castle. Built on the top of mountain, Hearst filled this place with a treasure trove of European art to make a Conquistador blush. A monastery was transported from Spain stone by stone and reassembled in the complex. At parties worthy of the Great Gatsby, film stars, including Hearst's long-term mistress Marion Davies mingled with statesmen and financiers. 'In many ways, Pop was a medieval man,' says his son and heir, William Randolph Hearst Jr. 'He had a romantic vision of troubadours and trumpets, artists and ageless heroes, damsels and minstrels, and countless court jesters.'[1]

Like the radical journalists of the French Revolution, with whom Hearst certainly never compared himself, the American magnate failed to see any boundary line between newspapering and politics, sometimes running for office himself, or backing protégés when he didn't. In 1898, he did more than anyone else to precipitate war between Spain and the United States, a conflict which marked the emergence of the former colonies as a globally ambitious, imperial power. When the US battleship

13. William Randolph Hearst was the ultimate press baron, mixing politics, celebrity high life, and newspapering in a potent blend. Orson Welles based his film *Citizen Kane* on Hearst's life, but there is doubt about whether Hearst ever sent the famous message to one of his illustrators, telling him to stay in Cuba to cover a war that Hearst said he would ensure took place.

Maine sank in Havana Harbour, Hearst's papers falsely accused Spain of blowing it up. Before the fighting began, Hearst dispatched a well-known artist, Frederick Remington, to Havana to illustrate his reporters' dispatches. Remington, bored at the absence of death and destruction, cabled Hearst: 'Everything is quiet. There is no trouble here. There will be no war. I wish to return.' To which, Hearst's biographers record, the publisher replied: 'Please remain. You furnish pictures and I'll furnish war.' According to Hearst's son, this legendary reply was never uttered. It is perhaps fitting that the most famous exchange in journalistic history may have been a fiction.[2] That it is so well remembered owes everything to Citizen Kane, where the version sharpened by a Hollywood script writer reads: 'You provide the prose poems and I'll provide the war!'

This period also saw the rise of Hearst's great rival, Joseph Pulitzer, whose circulation battles led to the coining of the term 'Yellow Journalism', a reference to the bidding war between the two for the services of a popular cartoon strip character, the Yellow Kid. Pulitzer's name lives on in American journalism's most coveted prizes.

In Britain, the dominant press baron of the period was Alfred Harmsworth, later Lord Northcliffe, who launched the *Daily Mail* in 1896, and at one time or another also owned *The Times*, the *Observer*, and the *Daily Mirror*. Like Hearst, Harmsworth was up to his neck in politics, seeking to manipulate opinion in Britain and the United States, though usually from an off-stage position. He believed that a newspaper had a unique ability to put its finger on the pulse of public opinion, by assessing its readers' correspondence, supplemented by the novel idea of conducting opinion surveys among readers. Winston Churchill wrote that during the Great War Northcliffe 'wielded power without official responsibility, enjoyed secret knowledge without the general view, and disturbed the fortunes of national leaders without being willing to bear their burdens'.[3] The quality of Northcliffe's intelligence, however, was far from flawless. In 1912, he declined an invitation to speak at an Albert Hall rally against votes for women with the comment that: 'I am one of those people who believe the whole thing to be a bubble, blown by a few wealthy women, who employ their less prosperous sisters to do the work. I judge public interest in the matter by the correspondence received. We never get any letters apart from those from the stage army of suffragettes.'[4]

Evelyn Waugh's comic masterpiece *Scoop* (1937) captured the world of Northcliffe and Beaverbrook in the fictional press baron, Lord Copper, whose erratic judgement was exceeded only by the stridency with which it was communicated. His terrified underlings, trying like all good journalists to stay just on the right side of the truth, developed a standard reply to his peremptory formulations which echoes through newsrooms to this day: 'Up to a point, Lord Copper.'

All industrialized countries had their Lord Coppers. In France, the textile manufacturer Jean Prouvost built a press empire which included the daily *Le Figaro, Paris-Soir*, and two of the twentieth century's most successful magazines, *Marie-Claire* for women and the illustrated weekly news magazine *Paris-Match*. In Germany, Spain, and Italy, matters were complicated by the rise and fall of fascism. Germany's biggest media group today, Bertelsmann, has its roots in religious book publishing in the nineteenth century, but the country's dominant newspaper owner, Axel Caeasar Springer, fitted the Citizen Kane bill, even though his firm only began operations in Hamburg in 1946, under licence from the occupying British forces. Springer launched the populist *Bild-Zeitung* in 1952 and by the mid-1960s controlled 40 per cent of the West German press. Like Hearst, Springer is famed for a single pronouncement—that too much reflection is bad for Germans—and is immortalized in a work of fiction, Heinrich Böll's *The Lost Honour of Katharina Blum*. In Italy, a media boss of the electronic age, Silvio Berlusconi, has managed to combine the office of prime minister with family control of the dominant commercial television provider, though Berlusconi argues that in practice he has no actual control over any part of the system.

But gradually, the corporate types have overhauled the tycoons, as the latter overreach themselves. AOL–Time Warner, Viacom, Vivendi, Bertelsmann, and Disney are run by professional managers, most with no background in news media. Even the American supermarket tabloids, once the personal instrument of extraordinary owner-publishers like Generoso Pope, are today mostly small units in large publishing groups. It is a matter of heated debate which of these models best serves journalism. In the heyday of press barons, journalists had a great deal to say about their bosses' excesses, prejudices, vanity, and occasional brutality. Italian journalists are hugely critical of the power wielded by Berlusconi and Rupert Murdoch's rise to power in the journalistic communities of Britain, the United States, and Australia has scarcely been without controversy.

Profits of Doom

Today, though, the main complaint of American journalists is directed against the shareholder-owned company, with its emphasis on quarter-to-quarter profits improvement and obsessive concern about share price. By incentivizing editors with share options and setting over-ambitious profits targets in response to Wall Street pressure, newspaper companies like Gannett and Knight Ridder are accused of weakening their titles' journalism and so damaging reader loyalty and the long-term future of the their business. 'By the end of the twentieth century, in deed if not in name, America's journalistic leaders had been transformed into businesspeople. And half now report that they spend at least a third of their time on business matters rather than journalism,'[5] argue leading lights in the influential Committee of Concerned Journalists.

Leonard Downie and Robert Kaiser, who work for the *Washington Post*, an organization whose formal statement of mission declares a willingness to sacrifice profit for service to its readers, have taken up this theme. Based on interviews with editors, past and present, across the country, they report that most of the 1,000 newspapers that serve American towns and cities 'are mediocre, many are much worse than that'. They accuse Gannett and Knight Ridder of demanding from their newsrooms soft features, friendly to local advertisers, rather than hard-hitting news stories, and illustrate the point with the example of a newspaper, the *Asbury Park Press*, which, following its takeover by Gannett, started charging its readers lineage for obituaries of family members, rather than seeing these as independently reported news items. Everywhere, they find journalists' jobs and expenses cut, even when advertising is strong, and savagely so during revenue downturns. 'I'm worried about American journalism,' says one editor, 'as we lose the independents, I wonder who's going to watch the government.' Gannett, they say, regularly moves editors and publishers around 'so they are relative strangers in the communities they serve'. Jay Harris, who resigned as publisher of the *San Jose Mercury News*, because his owners insisted upon cutting editorial expenses in order to boost already substantial profits, told fellow editors at a conference in 2001 that it was 'like watching a loved one commit suicide unintentionally'. In spite of all the smart new marketing techniques, and reader offers, sales of American newspapers fell throughout the 1990s. By 2000, only 55 per cent of American adults considered themselves regular newspaper readers, compared with 81 per cent in 1964.[6]

Murdoch, Last of the Big Beasts

How does this compare with, say, life on papers owned by one of the last great dynastic news barons, Rupert Murdoch, who inherited a newspaper business in Australia from his father and built it into a global media enterprise, incorporating the Fox television network and film business in the US, satellite television across four continents, HarperCollins the book publisher, and some of the most successful newspapers in the world, including Britain's top-selling titles, the *News of the World*, the *Sunday Times*, and the *Sun*? Murdoch, pictured on the front of the most widely used media studies textbook in Britain armed with a knife and fork to carve up a vulnerable planet earth, is portrayed as a modern Citizen Kane, capable of shaking governments in Washington, London, and Canberra before breakfast; a man who has found a way to do business with the latest regime in communist China as well as with whichever fly-by-night happens to be occupying the White House.

With Murdoch, the most frequently made charge is simply that he is too powerful, but this does need to be qualified. As Colin Seymour-Ure has pointed out, the 35 per cent share of the UK national newspaper market held by Murdoch's News International at the start of the twenty-first century was smaller than the proportion controlled by Lord Harmsworth a hundred years earlier. And during that same century, the BBC was constructed from scratch, and built for itself a 40 per cent share of the UK radio and television market—a level the competition authorities would never countenance for any private owner.

But Murdoch appears, in a way, content to play the bogeyman; perhaps it is the mischief-making journalist in him. When he arrived in Britain to take over the *News of the World* in 1969, he was asked whether he would interfere in the editorial operation. He hadn't, he replied, come to the other side of the world simply to sit back and watch. Murdoch demonology has him firing editors who will not do his bidding like a bored youth spitting out watermelon seeds and it is true that he has removed talented people who stood in his way, including the respected

14. Rupert Murdoch, last of the great press barons. In 1993, Murdoch said the days of the press magnate had gone, replaced by 'a bevy of harassed and sometimes confused media executives, trying to guess at what the public wants'.

Harold Evans, who quit the editor's chair at *The Times* live on the main evening television news in 1983, having been traduced by court politics following Murdoch's takeover of the loss-making *Times* and its hugely profitable sister paper, the *Sunday Times.* But it is not true to say that Murdoch has routinely operated a revolving door for editors at any of his newspapers. As he explained himself in an interview in 1999:

> If an editor is producing a paper you are basically pleased with and proud of and this is viable and doing well, then he is very safe in his job. If an editor is producing a paper which is clearly failing, turning the community against it, then you have to make changes. I've been in that position once or twice and been criticised for being ruthless in changing editors, but the people who'll be ruthless are the shareholders, who'll get rid of me if the papers go bust.[7]

Murdoch understates his clout among shareholders, over whom he has huge leverage because they are fragmented and he is not. But it is true to say that he is running a business which depends upon the support of lenders, shareholders, as well as readers. Murdoch, however, is an entrepreneur, a risk-taking visionary, who has more than once in a long career taken his financial backers to the brink.

No one much believed Murdoch when, in a speech in London in 1993, he announced that the day of the media mogul was done, but he was, more or less, right. 'The days when a few newspaper publishers could sit down and agree to keep an entire nation ignorant of a major event are long gone,' he said. 'Technology is racing ahead so rapidly, news and entertainment sources are proliferating at such a rate, that the media mogul has been replaced by a bevy of harassed and sometimes confused media executives, trying to guess at what the public wants.'[8]

Multimedia Loses Sight of Journalism

The truth is that it is difficult to generalize about the ownership conditions that make a great newspaper possible. Tom Rosenstiel of the Committee of Concerned Journalists, insists that

> the biggest change is that journalism is no longer produced primarily by companies engaged mostly in journalism. For example, Time Inc was once a company that generated all of its revenues from producing magazines and other kinds of journalism. By the time Time Inc merge with Warner Communications, about 50 per cent of its revenues came from journalism. With the merger between Time Warner and AOL, journalism became less than five per cent of revenues, although the company controls 35 per cent of all the magazine circulation in the United States. So a major part of magazine journalism in the US is a tiny part of this giant conglomerate. The values of the people who run

that company are very different. These are not journalists in the sense that Henry Luce (*Time*'s founder) was.[9]

Yet the same could have been said of the ownership of the *Financial Times* in the 1970s and 1980s, when it was starting to emerge as one of the great global newspapers.

Nor does journalism always prosper inside family-owned companies, which often run out of willpower and capital, making them easy prey for the larger newspaper groups in any period of rapid, capital-intensive technological change. Today, there are many great newspapers that are owned by public companies, among them the *Wall Street Journal* and the *New York Times.* Equally, there are world-class papers owned by families or trusts (the *Guardian* and the *Washington Post*), just as there are truly great news media organizations within the public sector, of which the BBC is a notable example.

Newspapers in Trouble

The inescapable reality with newspapers is that everywhere they are struggling to maintain circulation and share of advertising revenues against growing electronic competition. Although newspapers will be with us for a long time to come, television and radio have eaten away at their display advertising and new electronic media have dealt two blows: siphoning off some classified job, property, and car advertising and extending the practice of making news free at the point of the consumption.

Even this point, however, must be qualified. Before the arrival of computerized typesetting technology in the 1970s, and when electronic media competition was less intense, Britain's national newspapers still managed to be chronically unprofitable, bywords for outdated management and disastrous labour relations. Thirty years later, they had invested in new technology, but still managed to burn most of their cash in price wars or by competing with each other to add additional weekend supplements. The fact that sales were continuing to fall, especially among the tabloids, intensified these competitive pressures. In the regional press, sales of daily newspapers continued to fall sharply in the 1990s, encouraging steady consolidation into larger groups, which struggled like their American counterparts to satisfy the performance criteria of financial markets. Between 1945 and 1995, the number of morning titles published outside London fell by a third and the survivors struggled to hold circulation. Just as American cities became one-newspaper towns, in this period cities that had enjoyed the services of two evening newspapers were reduced to single title, though the total number of provincial evening newspapers fell only slightly, to sixty-eight.[10] Weekly local papers have fared rather better, though they have been hurt by the growth in circulation of free newspapers, which are mostly today owned by publishers of paid for titles. The resulting pressure has been reflected, inevitably, in editorial resources.

Does media ownership by powerful individuals create a greater risk of corrupt influence-peddling than wider corporate ownership? Again, there is no hard and fast answer. Certainly, a Rupert Murdoch or a Randolph Hearst have both stood to gain commercially from their ability to influence major political questions. In Britain, for example, the Blair government has been widely perceived to live in fear of the Murdoch press's opposition to British membership of the European currency, having learnt in eighteen years of opposition the extent to which papers like the *Sun* could expose its political enemies to mockery. Murdoch's own Euroscepticism is, at least partly, based upon his resistance to EU constraints upon an open global market in media content.

TV Journalism Bought Out

But other forms of corporate ownership also entail problems, especially when the companies involved become very large, using their power in one medium to promote their interests in another and, as a result, denying media access to their commercial rivals. As the American networks have settled into ownership by global entertainment companies, their news programmes have been caught out giving handsome coverage to the latest movie blockbuster from the parent company and ignoring a rival company's new release. But this is not a problem confined to shareholder-owned media companies: the BBC constantly cross-trails programmes and other services, sometimes on its news programmes. A recent example was an item on a news show about a new record from a popular band, Oasis, which urged viewers to tune in to a BBC entertainment show later that same day. The item was treated as a kind of 'news' and given the benefit of a three-minute critical discussion. The same thing happens all the time with cross-trailing from news to sports events owned by the broadcaster. These examples may seem trivial, but they are not so to commercial companies seeking to compete with the BBC. The BBC's commercial news rivals accuse the corporation of supplying news services to certain distributors either free or at prices which do not reflect the costs of the service.

Occasionally, these conflicts of interests by media owners develop into full-blown scandal. CBS, for example, was shown to have pulled its punches on an investigation into the tobacco industry, at the time when its owner was negotiating a takeover deal in the same industry. Journalists cried foul and Hollywood gave the story full feature treatment, resulting in Michael

Mann's 1999 film, *The Insider*, starring Al Pacino and Russell Crowe.

If it is agreed that all forms of media ownership can lead to behaviour which is institutionally self-serving or even corrupt, the best defence is to make sure that we do not depend too heavily upon any single owner or type of owner, which points to the need for national and international laws to limit concentration of media ownership. Today, there is great anxiety that we may be witnessing the emergence of an unprecedented global oligopoly, operating in media markets all over the world, and capable of dominating markets for distribution and content rights.

Ownership Concentration: Myth and Reality

It is not, in truth, wholly clear that this is the case, at least not yet. The most comprehensive study of the situation in the United States, for example, showed that there had been 'only modest shifts in the role of major players in the media industry between 1980 and 1998'.[11] This is, in part, because laws which resist media concentration have caused firms to dispose of some interests, as they acquire new ones. That pressure to re-fragment after consolidation may also partly explain why only a third of the companies that made the list in 1980 were still present in 1998. The most salient characteristic of modern media ownership is not its concentration, but its instability. The authors of this study conclude that the US media industry is 'one of the most competitive major industries in the US'.[12] They go on to say that 'in the world of unlimited virtual bandwidth, the curse of who owns the media may be in its unwieldy anarchy rather than in the feared controlled oligopoly'.[13] Even News Corporation's buying up of local television stations in the US, a notorious act of media concentration, enabled Fox to create a fourth television network, creating greater competition for ABC, CBS, and NBC, which may itself result in the combination of the networks to defend their diminishing market share.

The desire to resist excessive media concentration remains a lively and proper political concern in most countries, on the grounds that plurality of ownership is more likely to lead to diversity of editorial approach, though plurality itself does not guarantee diversity since the media are great imitators of each other. Also, weighed against the goal of plurality is an increasing governmental focus upon the need for national media companies to do well in international markets, so strengthening their contribution to the home country's performance in the so-called 'knowledge economy'. This tension between culture and commerce, or democracy and industrial development, is likely to intensify in the coming years.

In practice, methods to resist media concentration have taken many different forms. In Scandinavia, for example, government provides subsidies to newspapers threatened with closure in situations where the result would be monopoly publishing. The US Congress, in 1970, passed the Newspaper Preservation Act, designed to resist the economic forces leading to the closure of second newspapers in American towns and cities. One of its measures involved allowing rival companies to share plant and other overheads, so long as they preserved titles under separate ownership and editorial control. The law's impact, however, was less marked than its advocates hoped. By the late 1990s, only thirty-four cities had two newspapers, compared with more than 500 in the 1920s.

This rapid consolidation, however, was in some senses counterbalanced by the very rapid growth in the magazine business, serving a huge variety of specialized tastes, as well as in general interest magazines. Between 1950 and 1998, the number of magazine titles almost doubled, from 6,600 to 11,800. Book publishing also flourished, though remarkably there are no accurate data on the number of titles published in the United States each year.[14]

Concerns about diminished plurality of ownership also must be set alongside the growth in electronic media. In Britain, in the last decade, the number of commercial radio stations has grown from 50 to 250 and television offers more than 200 channels, compared with four or five a decade ago. All of these media offer some sort of news service, with the result that the total volume of television news on offer to British viewers in multi-channel homes increased roughly eightfold during the 1990s.[15] British television, however, has so far failed to achieve the localness of news service provided by a good newspaper and most of the emphasis in radio's growth has been in music radio. In Britain, these commercial radio stations are all served by a central news provider, Independent Radio News, whose output they receive in effect free. Their lack of interest in news and political life was demonstrated during the general election in 2001, when only a dozen of these 250 stations were willing to involve their listeners in a a live phone-in with Tony Blair, the prime minister, and his rivals for office. Commercial radio news, which tends to be short, increasingly emphasizes entertainment and sport ahead of politics or foreign news.

More News, Fewer Owners?

It is another paradox of modern news media that there is so much worry about the decline of our news media at a time when we have never had so much news available from so many suppliers. Satellite television and the internet have made overseas news sources easily accessible to ordinary citizens for the first time and a number of broadcasting organizations have made significant investments in 24-hour news. Although there is evidence in most advanced countries that younger people are less interested in both news and politics than their predecessor generations, and that they read fewer newspapers, it is not established whether, as a result, they know less about what's going on. It may be that news has become so ubiquitous, infiltrating our mobile phones, work stations, cars, and public spaces that headline news at least is being absorbed like the air we breathe. News has, as argued earlier in this book, become ambient, or as a young man told us in a focus group inquiring into news usage in Britain in 2002, 'news is something which grabs you. You don't need to grab it.'

None of this will necessarily make governments significantly more relaxed about concentrations of media ownership or incursions by foreign media owners into their own territories. Many countries continue to prohibit foreign ownership of television, which is why Rupert Murdoch had to become an American citizen in order to take over Fox television. Under European Union law, EU countries are not allowed to discriminate against fellow member countries, but most EU countries still restrict media ownership by non-European firms. Britain, unusually and amid some controversy, is in the process of abolishing its controls on foreign ownership on the grounds that the government believes the resulting stimulus to investment will be good for the media sector's development. Almost all countries also place restrictions on the extent to which corporations can combine interests in newspapers, television, and radio.

Businesses tend to argue that concentration of ownership should be regulated in exactly the same way for the media as it is for other businesses, on the grounds of excessive market power, but with the news media there are added complexities. Product markets with three or four competitors might well be sufficient to prevent price gouging and other practices unfriendly to consumers, but with the news media, there is a widespread sense that the restrictions need to be tighter on cultural and democratic grounds.

Europe's Defences

Nowhere have these tensions been felt more strongly than in Europe, where individual countries have constructed an apparatus of rules, cultural barriers, or other forms of intervention designed to ensure diversity of media ownership. Although a wide-ranging European Union 'Television without Frontiers' directive was watered down in the 1980s by resistance from the liberalizing British government of Margaret Thatcher, in practice Europe's journalism market has remained heavily defended.

In the end, economic and political factors trade off against each other in media ownership. Politicians have an interest in securing leverage over the news media, which is one of the reasons they have been so keen to maintain television as a highly regulated industry. Citizens' interest may point in the direction of highly fragmented ownership, on the grounds of extending choice, but this may mean news media lack the resources to invest in quality staff and equipment. We need to regulate the news media without stifling them; to protect a valued inheritance, without closing it off from the pressures of market-driven innovation.

Keep the Customer Satisfied

In pursuing a balance of this kind, there is no better reference point than the satisfaction of the public. So far as can be discerned, the British public is not discontented with a situation where a rather polemical, profit-seeking press competes with itself and against a broadcasting sector dominated by the BBC, which is itself subject to competition from smaller commercial players, which are also regulated in the public interest. How the law should then respond to the fact that the internet has turned the BBC into a large-scale producer of text-based news, in which domain it competes with unregulated newspaper internet sites, is something with which politicians and regulators will have to struggle, just as they will have to decide how to respond to dramatic changes in the ability to distribute television, as broadband networks develop.

Do Journalists Care Who they Work for?

These, then, are some of the political and policy perspectives. But what about the journalists? What do they say, if you ask them, about the types of organization for which they work? The answer is that they are inclined to grumble a lot, whoever is boss. Journalism is, at root, a highly individualistic occupation, especially on newspapers, and ethical responsibility lies as much with the individual journalist as with any institutional framework. This explains why, despite countless attempts, journalists have not been good at forming powerful professional associations to regulate their own professional standards or even, in many countries, at running effective trade unions.

Having worked myself for a British shareholder-owned company (Pearson); a publicly owned corporation (the BBC); a proprietor-owned magazine (the *New Statesman*) and a newspaper owned by a mixture of British, Irish, Italian, and Spanish shareholders (the *Independent*), I would not say that one 'model' is preferable to another. Outstanding journalism was done in all these settings and each had its weaknesses. At the BBC, there was a sense of a great tradition of public service, and genuine concern at every level for accuracy and fairness, but there was also hefty bureaucracy and a culture which militated against risk-taking. You would not want to live life only with journalism produced by an institution like the BBC: it would be too cautious, too dull. Working for the *Financial Times*, the atmosphere was intellectually bracing and wonderfully international. But it could also be deadeningly narrow. Every year, there was a competition for the dullest headline on the paper and there was never a shortage of entries. For some inexplicable reason, it is the one about unchanged levels of anchovy catches off the Peruvian coast which has stuck in my memory. The *Financial Times*, at its worst, is capable of reducing a cataclysm on any scale to its effects upon world stock markets.

The Editor's Life

After fifteen years at the *FT*, I became editor of the *Independent* during a period of the purest madness, when the paper was lurching from widely held ownership towards a more secure resting place in Tony O'Reilly's Dublin-based Independent group. By the time I got to the paper in 1994, Rupert Murdoch had launched a price war in the broadsheet market designed to kill us off and we were managed by ex-Murdoch executives from the Caligula school of management. They were themselves constantly plotting against the other shareholders, but still had the power to order me to cut the editorial budget by a third, and then, as soon as I had done so, by almost the same amount again, at which point I declined and was relieved of my duties. But somehow, in the middle of it all, writers continued to produce great pieces, to which readers reacted. In the late afternoon of a particularly bloody day I shut the door of my office, looking west from the Canary Wharf tower, and wrote an editorial parodying a Shakespeare play. I can't remember its subject, or even the name of the play, but the letter I got from a reader saying that it was reassuring to know the paper's sense of humour and style was in such sound health stands out as a high point in a tough period. The *New Statesman* also involved a sense of close contact with readers, many of whom worked in or around Parliament and so within a mile of the magazine's offices. Our entire editorial team at the *Statesman* never exceeded eight, which meant the editor had to do a great deal of coaxing to get good writers to contribute to the magazine at a fraction of their normal rates of pay.

What an editor needs to do the job well is enough money to hire writers, reporters, editors, graphic artists, and photographers; freedom to take editorial decisions and as much managerial stability and support as possible. The task often seemed to me to be comparable to that of managing a football club: exciting, turbulent, and hugely rewarding when things were going your way. If you lost the support of your boss, the owner, chief executive, or chairman, then there was no point staying around to discuss the rights and wrongs. 'It's only a question of when, not if, you get the boot,' Kelvin Mackenzie, the former

Sun editor, told me in the back of a taxi one day during my tenure at the *Independent*. 'It's the same with politicians. It has to come to a forced end.'

When a strong, inventive editor happens to coincide with stable ownership and shrewd business management, great things are possible. But these conditions can arrive, or not, in any system of ownership. Utopian forms of worker control do not achieve much if the advertising department cannot sell space. What readers, viewers, and listeners need is a diversity of models, along with a diversity of owners. France's *Le Monde*, for example, is one-third owned by its journalists. The *Guardian* is owned by a non-profit trust. Shareholder-owned and proprietor-owned news media are fine in the mix, so long as they do not drive out all the alternatives. It does matter who owns journalists, but it is not the only thing that matters: journalism, if it is any good, is chiefly concerned with the world beyond itself. Adam Michnik, editor-in-chief of *Gazeta Wyborcza*, refused to accept share options in what became an increasingly powerful publishing group in post-cold war Poland on the grounds that, as editor, he felt he should measure himself not by the growth in shareholder value, but by the service provided to readers. Agora, the company which owns the newspaper, also set up a charitable trust to hold 7.5 per cent of its stock when it was successfully floated on the stock market in

1999. 'This isn't just a business for us,' said Wanda Rapaczynski, chief executive of Agora, 'part of being a free media, untainted by political interests, is being willing to play a role in the country's democracy. And part of that belief is being committed to broad ownership of this company and giving back to our country.'[16] Does Agora offer a model? Not really. But an admirable example? Certainly.

Editors and their owners do also, sometimes, face intractable difficulties. When, in 1996, I went to edit the *New Statesman*, a weekly political magazine created by George Bernard Shaw, the Webbs, and other Fabians in the 1920s, it had just been bought by Geoffrey Robinson, a businessman and Labour Member of Parliament. Robinson was an ideal owner in that he invested generously in the business and kept out of editorial decisions. On one occasion, Clare Short, an outspoken figure in Tony Blair's shadow ministerial team, made a high-risk attack upon the spin doctors, 'people in the dark' surrounding the Labour leader. After going to press, I phoned Robinson to warn him of the row that would soon engulf the magazine. He was on holiday in Kenya. Having heard an account of the interview he replied: 'From where I am standing, I can see a lioness approaching. It's really quite remarkable here.' It was the end of the conversation. Later, during his time as Treasury minister, a more serious matter arose. Robinson's business affairs were the subject of official investigation. What should the *New Statesman* do? Pile in with its own investigations? Defend him or give him space to defend himself? I felt we would not be trusted if we took either course, so we explained to our readers that this was a story we would leave to others, an action which led to a public denunciation by a previous *New Statesman* editor in the next available edition of the *Guardian*.

These, of course, are perspectives from British journalism. For editors and reporters in many parts of the world, daily life is physically dangerous and always tense. Journalists are frequently intimidated, prosecuted, jailed, attacked, and killed. As editor of the *Independent*, I was myself the subject of a criminal prosecution following our decision to publish leaked material from a court case, which revealed government duplicity in the overseas sale of armaments. I could have gone to jail, but I didn't seriously think I would. It is easy to underestimate the courage needed to be a journalist in many parts of the world, where the the threat of jail, or worse, is real.

As for the latest generation of global media players, it is too early to be sure what they will bring to the character of their news media interests. The danger may be less unfair or corrupt behaviour of this or that owner, but the possibility that the economics of news no longer work in a modern media business context. Greg Dyke, the director general of the BBC, in

2002 speculated that American television networks might even consider withdrawing from the news business altogether: 'I had lunch fairly recently with the guy who runs ABC News in the States, and he said "if there's a future for ABC News . . ." That was inconceivable a decade ago. All the American networks have discovered that their news no longer makes them money. That reality, that commercial reality has hit in Britain.'[17]

Express Train to Nowhere

The problem is that good journalism costs money, while the financial return from journalism is highly uncertain. Take the fate of a single newspaper group. In the last thirty-five years, the *Daily Express* and the *Sunday Express*, Beaverbrook Newspapers, have been owned, serially, by a property company, Trafalgar House, United Newspapers, MAI, a financial services conglomerate, and a small publishing group that made much of its fortune from pornography. In that period, sales of the daily newspaper have fallen from roughly four million to below one million. Andrew Cameron has spent his entire working life on the business side of newspapers and was managing director of Express Newspapers from 1986 to 1996, before he was fired by MAI. This is how he sums up his understanding of the way that newspapers work:

The Express titles were at their most successful in former years when they catered for their readers, not only the bean-counters. Editorial is rightly the major cost centre of a newspaper. You risk the performance and credibility of your publication by employing low paid, inexperienced journalists. Quality comes from good writers, and from good exclusives bought for fair sums and with good judgment. Quality does not come by reducing freelance rates nor by employing a 'hot desk' policy. Quality is about people; newspapers are about people.[18]

It is impossible to quarrel with this judgement. There is a creative magic about newspapers, and indeed about all news media, which is not susceptible to management formula or reorganization by business consultants. Journalism today is in peril not because one type of ownership has taken precedence over another, but because owners of all shapes and sizes are in danger of losing sight of this rather basic point, that journalism is always about something larger than a commercial relationship between a publisher and a customer. Journalism raises issues for business which go beyond routine business considerations. Just as it does for governments, as Colin Seymour-Ure argues:

Increasingly, governments recognized that media complexity was a problem. More difficult was the decision what the problem was. In the days when media concentration meant little more than the gathering of several national papers in the hands of a Northcliffe or a Kemsley, the argument could be conducted in the language of party policies and monopoly capitalism. But when the term media itself was loose at the edges (not to mention the crumbling edges of the nation state), the game was more three-dimensional chess than flat-earth draughts.[19]

The idea of the public, and public opinions, from which journalism derives its legitimacy, is becoming ever more demanding. Lord Coppers, present and future, please note.

5

Hacks v. Flaks

Journalism and Public Relations

Of the many self-indulging aphorisms beloved of journalists, one of the most comforting states: 'News is something somebody somewhere doesn't want printed. All the rest is advertising.' Often attributed to Lord Northcliffe, the British press baron, it is easy to see why this breezy over-simplification exerts such appeal, portraying the journalist as crusader, single-mindedly engaged in exposing truth against all the odds. The quotation pops up all over the place: it was, for example, taken as a mission statement by a news website[1], contrasting the value of its own information, paid for by reader subscription, with news tainted by association with public relations people, advertisers, or sponsors.

The Northcliffe doctrine, if that is what it is, raises one of the central issues in journalism, namely, in whose interests does the journalist work: for the company or organization with employs him or for a wider public good? And if journalists in a commercial setting are primarily working for their shareholders' profits, or the esteem of their own organization, can they legitimately draw such a sharp distinction between the value and plausibility of their own work and other forms of so-called 'commercial speech', namely the information put out to the public directly by organizations through their own channels of public communications or public relations?

The more that journalism resembles mere entertainment, the harder this question bites and the more difficult it becomes to defend, let alone advance, the privileges democratic societies afford journalists: such as the right not to reveal sources of information; and the right, subject to laws of libel and contempt, to free expression.

The Northcliffe doctrine appeals to journalists because it cheerily evades such complexities. According to it, news cannot come from PR men. It must be hard-won. Anything which arrives in a press release, or in the form of an official announcement, or even as official guidance, is at best worthless and most likely a lie. As the journalist Claud Cockburn once said: 'Never believe anything until it is officially denied.' Public relations is an occupation for smooth-talking twisters or moronic sand-baggers.

Mau-mau the flak-catchers

Tom Wolfe captured the spirit of the matter in his report of life in San Francisco's poverty programme in 1970. Wolfe's portrait of the shifty, shabby 'flak-catcher' captures the official spokesman with nothing at his disposal but hollow words, confronted or 'mau-maued' by an angry, multiracial group demanding to know why their subsidized job scheme is to be cut back. Wolfe writes:

> This lifer is ready to catch whatever flak you're sending up. It doesn't matter what bureau they put him in. It's all the same. Poverty, Japanese imports, valley fever, tomato-crop parity, partial disability, home loans, second-probate accounting, the Interstate 90 detour change order, lockouts, secondary boycotts, GI alimony, the Pakistani quota, cinch mites, Tularemic Loa loa, veterans' dental benefits, workmen's compensation, suspended excise rebates—whatever you're angry about, it doesn't matter, he's there to catch the flak. He's a lifer.[2]

The uncomfortable fact for journalists today, one hundred years since the birth of the public relations industry, is that there are in the United States more flak-catchers (or 'flaks' as reporters sometimes call them) than journalists (or hacks, as journalists sometimes call themselves). And where the US leads in such matters, others tend to follow.[3] Nor do today's flak-catchers merely or mainly block the hacks' flak: they pre-empt it, see it coming, and get the journalists, wherever they can, to see matters their way. The fear among journalists is that they no longer have the resources to counter the increasingly sophisticated munitions of their traditional enemy: that journalism is being hung out to dry by the not-so-hidden persuaders.

It is true that public relations people, especially those working in the upper reaches of financial, corporate, and government public relations, are better paid than all but a handful of very senior or celebrity journalists; they also frequently have access to better technology and support systems. Some would say, but this is more controversial, that they are also better disciplined, more professional, and more skilful, and that this is the main reason journalism is in danger of being outsmarted. 'The trouble with journalism today,' one senior public relations executive told me, 'is that the journalists we deal with tend to be rather young, not very experienced and stretched by the number of deadlines they're running against. You often feel that you are dealing with people who really don't understand the story. That's quite scary.' Anyone who has been on the receiving end of a journalist's enquiries will recognize an element of truth in this: there is nothing quite so terrifying as the knowledge that someone is about to tell a few million people about yourself or your organization without understanding it or, sometimes, even taking the trouble to try. In such circumstances a reporter's well-informed scepticism, even prejudiced hostility, is greatly to be preferred to self-satisfied ignorance and laziness.

Journalists are also less than honest when they pretend that they do not make use of public relations contacts and other official sources of information. They will want to swagger, with

Claud Cockburn, but in reality, journalists use any source of information they can tap. A journalist covering any beat naturally wants access to top people: the decision takers and primary sources. But this is not always realistic: top people are, by definition, too busy to spend all day on the phone to journalists, so they surround themselves with intermediaries, whose job it is to deal with the news media that operate around the clock, around the year. Skilled reporters also recognize that there is a hierarchy of sources for information and that you don't go to your top contacts for routine facts, or to check history.

Lazy Journalism

But lazy journalists and thinly resourced newspapers, trade magazines, or broadcast newsrooms do become overdependent upon these intermediaries, often reproducing gratefully whatever ready-made material comes their way. The quickly sub-edited press release, or even the non-edited version, can be inspected any day in thousands of publications. Free newspapers and smaller commercial radio stations often operate with few or even no reporters; they publish only what someone sends in. As long ago as the 1950s, Scott Cutlip attempted to calculate the proportion of American news column inches taken up with information supplied by public relations practitioners. His conclusion was that nearly half of what we read came via this route.[4]

And that was before the dramatic increase in the scale of US public relations industry in the last forty years of the century, and the corresponding decline in editorial resources on many newspapers. No wonder the information we get from the news media is so uniform, to the point where there is even a genre of journalism which seeks to summarize all the others: publications such as *The Week* or the *Guardian*'s, '*The Editor*'. The latter runs a very effective service summarizing in a couple of hundred words the essential core of the dozens of interviews pumped out by the public relations machine of, say, an artist releasing a new record, or a writer publishing a new book. With the growth of the internet, readers today also have the choice of going directly to the artist's website, to read the public relations message unmediated.

Today, public relations professionals hand out not only press releases, but photographs, CD-ROM images, audio and video clips. The top PR firms video their clients' public events and webcast them, to be picked up by journalists, or for direct consumption by interested parties, underlining another way in which the internet makes it even harder to distinguish journalism from other forms of commercial speech. There was controversy in the 1980s when the BBC used video supplied by the environmental campaign group Greenpeace, on the grounds that it was not 'independent' material. Today, broadcasters frequently use video material supplied by a huge range of sources. Some take more care than others in checking and labelling its provenance. Organizations like Greenpeace see their media strategy as encompassing the creation of attractive, multimedia information services, distributed direct to supporters: they no longer have to rely entirely upon the mass media. Even the British royal family has a series of websites, which are used to rebut what they regard as misleading reports in the newspapers.

Meanwhile, some of what appears in the mass media as journalism needs to be questioned. Many newspapers and magazines, including some of the most respectable, publish 'advertorials,' often written by the same journalists who write other news and features. Are these features, commissioned only because they have the support of specific advertisers or sponsors, really journalism assembled without fear or favour? The truth is that some are more honest and honourable than others. Many are a disgrace. Claud Cockburn may have had his tongue in cheek when he said: 'the journalist is partly in the entertainment business and partly in the advertising business', but he was not entirely wrong.

Enter the Spin Doctor

The growth of public relations machinery has caused special concern in the field of politics, with the emergence of the political 'spin-doctor' in American politics in the 1980s and since then almost everywhere else. This phenomenon is blamed by politicians upon the fact that the newspapers themselves no longer separate fact and comment and 'spin' against the politicians, leaving the politicians with no choice but to respond in kind. Whoever is to blame, there is no doubt that these practices are one cause of growing public cynicism about the purposes of politics and may even have contributed to the steady and alarming decline in public participation in elections. One spin-doctor in Tony Blair's government was forced to resign when it was revealed that she had sent an email on the day of the terrorist attacks on New York and Washington in September 2001, pointing out that this would be a good day 'to bury some bad news' about local government expenditure.

And the Market-Fixer

Politics, however, is not the only area where the activities of journalists and public relations people threaten to collide in explosive fashion. In business and financial markets, unscrupulous public relations professionals circulate information, often false or half-false, but designed to raise the stock prices of companies for which they work, a task which often involves the collusion of investment bankers, stock analysts, and a swathe of people who straddle the line between investment advice, salesmanship, and journalism. Since the collapse of stock markets in 2001/2, these practices have attracted the attention of financial market regulators around the world, some of whom have moved to make rules which require journalists and other media players to identify their financial interests when pontificating in print or on air. 'The world of Wall Street spin is more like a dozen simultaneous games of three-dimensional chess, a daily, dizzying match in which stock prices, corporate earnings, and millions of individual investments are riding on the outcome', says Howard Kurtz, media reporter for the *Washington Post.* 'In this overheated environment, the degree to which basic facts can be massaged, manipulated, and hyped is truly troubling. And that raises the fundamental question: amid the endless noise, whom do you trust?'[5]

Whom indeed. From whichever direction you approach the intertwined worlds of journalism and public relations, trust is the critical issue. Should the public's working assumption be that any unmediated message, from a politician, government department, non-governmental organization, or business is either a lie or self-serving half-truth, the impression often given by journalists? If so, can they make the assumption that journalists have the integrity to test and interrogate rival claims, serving a general public interest? As we saw in Chapter 2, opinions surveys suggest that journalists are as little trusted to tell the truth as politicians and business people. Some modesty, on the part of journalists, is in order.

It is not a coincidence that the history of journalism and public relations is very closely connected. Some of the great figures in modern journalism's earliest days, also operated as paid agents for powerful interests. And, in the last hundred years, journalists, or ex-journalists, have created the modern public relations industry and continue to supply much of its expertise.

How Journalists Created the PR Industry

The first recognizable public relations agency was born in Boston in 1900, but the idea of 'persuasive speech' is at least as old as Plato. Classical notions of *vox populi, vox dei* point to the emergence of public opinion as something whose significance rulers are obliged to recognize. 'Not without reason is the voice of the people compared to the voice of God,' wrote Machiavelli, leaving rulers with the choice of whether to 'caress or annihilate' the owners of those voices. The word propaganda has its origin in the seventeenth-century Roman Catholic Church's 'Congretatio de Propaganda Fide', literally aimed at propagating the faith.[6]

Public relations emerged as an aspect of modern industrial management in the early 1900s as the United States engaged in one of its periodic backlashes against excessive business power.

This was the age of President Theodore Roosevelt and the trust-busters, who broke up the vast, monopolistic empires of John D. Rockefeller and others. It was Roosevelt's ally Gifford Pinchot who remarked, presciently, that 'nothing permanent can be accomplished in this country unless it is backed by sound public sentiment'. Rockefeller was among the first American business leaders to recognize the importance of trying to shape public opinion in favour of his business objectives, and to counter the influence of a growing army of 'muck-raking' journalists. Notable among the 'muck-rakers' was the writer Upton Sinclair, who exposed the filth and corruption of the country's meat-processing industry. Soon, every self-respecting business had a team of lawyers to deal with the competition authorities and professional communicators to promote its cause with journalists and the public. The obvious place to recruit these communicators was from newspapers.

William Wolff Smith was still a reporter for the *Baltimore Sun* when he opened his 'publicity business' in Washington in 1902 and he continued to operate as a 'stringer' or part-time correspondent for a number of newspapers, while supplying pieces reflecting the views and interests of his clients. Smith also, like many of his successors, had a long-running relationship with the tobacco industry, whose journal he supplied with regular intelligence from the nation's capital.

Rockefeller's first public relations 'counsellor', as he liked to be called, was Ivy Ledbetter Lee, son of a Methodist preacher from Georgia, and a former police reporter on Hearst's *New York Journal*. Lee joined the Rockefeller payroll in 1914, following his skilful work in handling the aftermath of the company's bloody assault against striking Colorado mine-workers and their families (the 'Ludlow Massacre') the previous year. One of the radical journalists who reported the massacre, George Creel, would also go on to make his own name in another branch of public relations, chairing the path-breaking Committee on Public Information, which sought to unite public opinion at home and propagandize on behalf of the United States abroad during the First World War. After the Armistice, Creel's vast programme released into the American private sector a demobbed army of public relations experts, who built the modern public relations industry. Edward Bernays, a sometime reporter and Broadway theatrical press agent, worked for the Creel committee, before starting his own agency in 1919, in partnership with his wife, Doris Fleischman. Eight years later, John Hill, another ex-newsman, opened an office in Cleveland, where he was soon joined by Don Knowlton to form Hill and Knowlton, one of the century's largest public relations firms.

Engineering Consent

Lee was clear that, for his techniques to succeed, his clients must deal plainly with the public: that they must show integrity in order to win trust. Only honest companies would meet 'the high demands of enlightened public sentiment'.[7] Others took the business even more seriously. Walter Lippman's seminal book *Public Opinion* appeared in 1922, recommending the application of social scientific techniques both to the measurement and shaping of public attitudes. Meanwhile Bernays, nephew of the psychologist Sigmund Freud, was setting himself up as the architect of modern public relations. His 1927 book *Crystallising Public Opinion* set out the novel idea that public relations was a two-way affair, which involved the professional PR 'counsel' shaping the behaviour of the client, as well as the attitude of the public. The blend of Freudian analysis and business acumen is captured in this extract from Bernays's statement of 'philosophy'

The counsel directs and supervises the activities of his clients wherever they impinge upon the daily life of the public. He interprets the client to the public and he interprets the public to the client. Perhaps the chief contribution of the public relations counsel to the public and to his client is his ability to understand and analyse obscure tendencies of the public mind. He first analyses his client's problem—he then analyzes the public mind.[8]

It was a short step from Bernays's pioneering thoughts to his concept of 'engineering consent' for an organization's goals. To some, this sounded too much like hypnosis and propaganda. They argued that the public relations practitioner had 'an ethical duty above that of his clients to the larger society'.[9] Barely out of its infancy, public relations was caught in a moral dialogue closely resembling the one still taking place today in journalism.

These loftier notions have, of course, encountered very many practical difficulties, as one PR firm or another has snatched at the cash, rather than pausing to ask any sort of ethical question. Ivy Lee, it turned out, was a paid adviser to I. G. Farben, the German chemical giant which was an accomplice in Hitler's attempted extermination of the Jews. Lee's career ended in shame.

Fakes and Other Mistakes

Not quite on the same scale, but probably more morally devious, were Hill and Knowlton's actions in the war which followed the invasion of Kuwait by Iraq in 1990. Employed by the Kuwaiti monarchy at a fee of $12 million to promote its interests inside the United States, the firm established a front organization called Citizens for a Free Kuwait. This, in turn, proceeded to manufacture stories about Iraqi atrocities in Kuwait, very much along the lines followed by British government propaganda in the First and Second World Wars. Nayriah, a sobbing 15-year-old girl, testified to a public hearing of Congress's Human Rights Caucus on 10 October 1990. She reported that she had seen Iraqi soldiers taking babies out of hospital incubators and leaving them 'to die on the cold floor'. Shortly afterwards, she was unmasked as the Washington-based daughter of the Kuwaiti ambassador. Hill and Knowlton also spent many years conveying the tobacco industry's case that its products were not to blame for lung cancer and other diseases. It was perhaps out of such hard-bitten pursuit of self-interest that John Hill, one of the firm's founders, advanced a less morally flamboyant definition of the goals of public relations as: 'the management function which gives the same organized and careful attention to the asset of good will as is given to any other major asset of the business.'[10]

Politics and PR

It was in the sphere of politics that public relations became most controversial. Hamilton Wright, whose early career included a spell on the *Los Angeles Times*, built the first public relations organization devoted to promoting the interests of overseas countries in the early 1900s. One of his techniques was to make a contractual guarantee to his clients that the money they paid him would buy at least five times as much publicity as the equivalent amount spent on advertising. Much later, in 1964, the

Public Relations Society of America censured the firm, now run by Wright's grandson, for violating one of its articles, which forbade pledging 'the achievement of specified results beyond a member's direct control'.[11] But the accused man simply quit the society and carried on business as usual, illustrating another similarity between public relations and newspaper journalism: namely its resistance to any form of truly independent regulation.

The more momentous change was in the use of modern public relations as a technique of domestic political communication. In 1930s California, two ex-reporters, the husband and wife team of Clem Whitaker and Leone Baxter, came together to fight and win a local referendum. After this success, they formed a firm, Campaigns, Inc, the first professional campaign consultants, a breed which has dominated every American election campaign since. In Whitaker's own words, they transformed campaign management from being 'a hit or miss business, directed by broken-down politicians' to being 'a mature, well-managed business founded on sound public relations principles, and using every technique of modern advertising'.[12]

Bill and Tony Go Large

The vigour of their legacy is today evident all over the world, in the rise of Bill Clinton to the presidency, the modernization of the British Labour Party, and the success of Tony Blair, which in turn influenced Gerhard Schroder's leadership of the German Social Democratic Party (SPD) and Lionel Jospin's of France's Socialist Party in the late 1990s. Philip Gould, a senior communications adviser to Tony Blair, has written extensively about the lessons he learnt from Clinton's New Democrats, recalling an especially momentous week at Clinton's campaign headquarters in Little Rock, Arkansas, in September 1992, just months after the British Labour Party had suffered yet another election defeat at the hands of the Conservative Party. 'This was a turning point for me in every way. It restored my faith and gave me the will to go on,' says Gould.[13] What crystallized for him in Little Rock was that a successful centre-left political strategy must appeal to the middle classes, rather than its natural blue-collar constituency, and that to do so it would have to adopt ruthlessly a new set of communications techniques, most of them learnt from business public relations and marketing. These included sophisticated data management to ensure instant rebuttal of hostile points; the centralized running of an election campaign from a single 'war room' according to a written 'war book'; the insistence that everyone involved in the campaign is 'on message' at all times, so that key lines are repeated time and again without self-contradiction; and the belief that campaigns are never-ending, rather than merely events which precede elections.

Any journalist exposed to the New Democrats' or New Labour's methods can testify to their zeal. A few weeks before the May 1997 general election, I was editing the *New Statesman*, a political magazine which had developed a reputation for springing stories picked up by other news media. One day, just before dispatching the final pages to the printer, I took a telephone call from the Labour Party's Millbank headquarters, to be told by a well-educated young voice: 'I'm calling from the Millbank Rapid Rebuttal unit. Could you tell me what you are putting in the magazine this week, so that I can prepare a rebuttal?'

Gould denies that the 'dark arts' of modern political campaigning, in which political enemies, sometimes within the same party, are smeared and false information trails promiscuously laid, are a departure from previous, well-established techniques or in any way ethically questionable. According to Gould, spin is

> a longstanding and completely unexceptional activity. In a world in which political parties, and other high-profile organizations, are under twenty-four hour media attack, it is common sense to employ people to put the view of the party or the organization and to do it to best effect. In a modern media environment, competence and good communications are inseparable: you cannot have one without the other.'[14]

15. In the 1990s President Bill Clinton invented and led the 'New Democrats' and Blair led 'New Labour.' Both perfected techniques of political communication ('spin') and other campaign methods which built upon techniques used in commercial public relations. By the turn of the century, these methods were controversial and, some said, counterproductive.

Gould is certainly right that Ivy Lee and John Hill were spin-doctors before Tony Blair was born. But these early public relations figures were operating in a world where the news media were less powerful and certainly less ubiquitous. Today, political life often appears to be a function of the media, a media phenomenon itself, as politicians dash from studio to studio, spending more time on television than they do in parliaments or Cabinet meetings. If it is true that the medium has become the message, as Marshall McLuhan foresaw, spin really does becomes the substance. Or, as McLuhan himself put it: 'the new media are not bridges between man and nature; they are nature'.[15]

Many British and American journalists certainly felt that the spin-doctors they dealt with in the 1990s had taken them into new territory, where the manœuvring became so duplicitous that journalists did indeed start to operate on the assumption that anything they were told by government was either a lie, a half-truth or a cunning manœuvre. In Britain, the Labour government after 1997 set about the task of reforming the government's communications machine, which traditionally operated outside the influence of party politics and tensions between New Labour and journalists reached new heights. No wonder the public started to feel as negative about the journalists as the politicians. The fact that Blair, by the time of his second landslide victory in 2001, was busily attempting to distance himself from the charge that his was a government of 'spin not substance' indicated that he was starting to understand the price paid for his apparent public relations triumph.

Money Makes the Spin Go Round

But it is not only the world of politics which has been turned upside down by its encounter with ubiquitous, 24-hours-a-day, instant news media. So too has the world of money. And here, unlike in politics, the effect of overstatement amplified by media competitiveness is more directly measurable. If the information journalists provide is wrong, markets can move, up or down, and fortunes and jobs can be created or destroyed.

During the extraordinary period between 1997 and 2001, when share prices soared in response to a period of wild over-optimism about the implications of new developments in communications technologies, journalism was itself being reshaped by the same communications revolution. All over the world, new web-based news and information services were being created, alongside an unprecedented range of television channels, many of which specialized in business, dividing their screens so that viewers could simultaneously observe an interview with a chief executive or a discussion between market analysts, and a constant stream of up to the second data.

By the turn of the century, a venerable firm like the news agency Reuters had been reinvented as a supplier of multimedia electronic market information to business and financial organizations; its global general news service survived, but was not the part of the business which drove profitability. Now Reuters had new competitors, like Bloomberg, which specialized in television-based business news and information and whose founder, Michael Bloomberg, became mayor of New York City in 2002: a reworking for the twenty-first century of the Citizen Kane myth.

By the late 1990s, the new TV channels and internet-based business news and comment services, such as thestreet.com, Jagnotes, and Marketwatch, were buoyed by booming markets. These new media businesses had themselves tapped the stock market for large sums of capital to support their rather shaky business plans. TheStreet.com, for example, went into partnership with the *New York Times* in the same period that Time – Warner considered, to its subsequent regret, that the internet firm America Online was a fitting equal partner with itself in a merger which amazed Wall Street. With markets booming, solo 'day traders' emerged all over the US, many of whom gave up regular, salaried jobs in the belief that they could make their fortunes on the stock market, buying and selling, now that the internet and television had given them access to information at a speed and quality found only inside an investment bank or stock brokerage house ten years earlier. One British journalist announced that he was giving up his own job to become a day trader, and chronicle his pathway to his first million. Amid this gold-rush, those who reported and commented on the market and individual stocks, whether live on television or via the World Wide Web, were seldom asked to make any disclosure about their own financial interests, though informed insiders knew full well that the expert Wall Street and City of London analysts employed by investment banks routinely issue nine 'buy' recommendations for every 'sell'.

One of the more extraordinary figures of this period was James Cramer, a millionaire Wall Street trader who combined the running of his own hedge fund for investors with a large stake in, and regular editorial appearances on TheStreet.com and that business's sister television show, which for a short period enjoyed a somewhat crazed existence on Rupert Murdoch's Fox News channel. Although it was editorial policy on thestreet.com for Cramer to declare his personal or professional interest in any stock mentioned in his commentaries, there were huge tensions in play. Was it legitimate for someone to be both a major private investor and a journalist serving his readers and viewers? In the same bull market, editorial dishonesty surfaced in more traditional news organizations as well. Journalists from the *Daily Mirror* in London and the *San Jose Mercury News* in the United States were caught lining their own pockets using information gathered in the course of their journalistic activities. Many expected the editor of the *Daily Mirror*, Piers Morgan, who had traded stock on the basis of his city desk's inside tips, to be fired, but he retained the support of the company that owns the paper, Trinity Mirror, enabling him to discover a new persona on the Damascus Road of 11 September. Suddenly the *Mirror* was again pursuing serious news, with a comment agenda strongly critical of the Bush and Blair administrations, consistent with its past as a campaigning, left-wing newspaper. In an apologia for past misdemeanours Morgan, who had edited the sleazy *News of the World* before becoming editor of the *Mirror*, said he now understood that 'Mirror readers didn't really hanker for the buckets of trashy, racy, celeb-driven scandal sleaze I was serving up. They wanted more substance. . . . The trivial stuff, whilst selling well on the day, was eroding loyal readers in the longer term.'[16]

Morgan's was not the only apologia as sobriety returned to Wall Street. Richard Lambert, editor of the *Financial Times* throughout the 1990s, acknowledged the failures of even the best business journalists in the world to spot and tell the world about the dubious business practices that started to come to light when the boom turned to crash at firms like Enron and Worldcom. 'The Enron affair reveals something about the culture of business journalism. As editor of the *Financial Times* over the period, I was part of the culture,' says Lambert. He notes that the signs of Enron's impending difficulties were, from the vantage point of the company's crash, 'there for anyone who cared to look'. Why did business journalists fail to spot them? 'Because they were too influenced by the views of big financial institutions, many of which rated Enron a 'buy' to the bitter end;

because too much business journalism today is concerned with personalities rather than hard analysis and because business, unlike politics, is largely conducted without transparency and behind the protection of fierce libel laws, especially in Britain. 'One of the main tasks of the media is to hold power to account. With no serious alternative to free market capitalism, governments are increasingly obliged to enter into relationships with corporations. An intelligent examination of business starts to become a crucial component of democratic choice.'[17] In these circumstances, it became rather difficult to say where salesmanship stopped and journalism began or to answer Howard Kurtz's question: 'amid the endless noise, whom do you trust?'

Trust Goes Bust

It all reminded me of the early days of the *Financial Times*, the London newspaper I worked on for fifteen years, and which spent decades building up its reputation as a trustworthy vehicle of financial news, against competition from other titles that allowed their reporters to moonlight as market traders. Today, the *FT*, like its serious competitors, has a register of journalists' investment interests and rules about the conditions which apply to any trading of stock. These rules, along with the fact that *FT* reporters and editors are paid salaries large enough to minimize the temptation for them to dabble dishonestly in the markets, are designed to consolidate that sense of trust between the *FT*, its sources of information, and its readers. In the paper's early days, there had been no such clarity. The paper's first chairman in 1888 was a 28-year-old publisher, Horatio Bottomley, whose subsequent career included the launch of a series of fraudulent companies on the back of the West Australian gold-rush. By 1922, the authorities had caught up with him and Bottomley was thrown into jail where a visiting acquaintance found him stitching mail bags. 'Ah, Bottomley, sewing?' enquired the visitor. 'No, reaping,' replied the *FT*'s founder.[18]

There is a powerful echo here with the world of political spin. In Philip Gould's own account of the rise of Tony Blair's New Labour, he turns to David Hill for a description of the spin-doctor's work. Hill, for many years the Labour Party's chief media spokesperson and a bridge between the worlds of 'old' and 'new' Labour, today works in commercial public relations. This is what he told Gould: 'You have to never tell a lie—telling lies is disastrous, because one of the most effective elements in being a spin-doctor is that they believe what you are saying to them. . . . Then you will have created a relationship with the journalists which is pivotal.'

It is the erosion of trust that has damaged modern politics, business, public relations, and journalism. Public relations and journalism are not the same as each other. Journalists should serve first and foremost the collective interest of their readers, listeners, and viewers, as well as serving the organization that employs them. With public relations people, it is the other way round. PR people are employed to serve the interests of the organization which employ them, but they can only do this effectively if they are trusted, which also requires plain-dealing and integrity. If, as Richard Lambert says, understanding business is a necessary aspect of a well-functioning modern democracy, quality communication between businesses and their stakeholders is essential. Here is the common moral nexus between journalism and other forms of public communications. Its betrayal undermines politics and markets. Without trust, politicians, business people, journalists, and public relations practitioners cannot do their jobs. These people are all in the same boat and perhaps they would row to better effect if everyone acknowledged that.

6

Murder is my Meat

The Ethics of Journalism

Journalism is a domain of moral choices, sometimes involving a melodramatic interplay between good and evil, which probably explains why the news media have proved such a fertile source of story-lines for Hollywood. Though not so popular as, say, police dramas or westerns, tales of crusading news hounds, compromised scandal sheet editors, and desperate-for-fame young TV reporters have done well at the box office from the film industry's earliest days. According to one authority, more than a thousand films have taken the news business as their central theme.[1]

Fictional news heroes and their ethical challenges come in many shapes and sizes, reflecting the dominant concerns of their day. In the 1930s, Torchy Blane, a female reporter, tested gender stereotypes in the urban jungle, demanding entry to a crime scene with the words: 'Holdups and murders are my meat. I'm Torchy Blane of the Star.'[2] Orson Welles's creation, *Citizen Kane*, based upon the career of William Randolph Hearst, delved into the news industry's hazy ability to discern the difference between fact and fiction. 'He was disappointed in the world, so he built one of his own,' says one of Kane's aides. This same decade also yielded the first of four screen adaptations of a successful Broadway play, *The Front Page* (1931), featuring Hildy Johnson's irrefutable description of the general news reporter's life: 'It's peeking through keyholes. It's running after fire engines, waking up people in the middle of the night. It's stealing pictures off little old ladies after their daughters get attacked.' In *Five Star Final* (1931) Edward G. Robinson publishes a paper that delights in ruining the lives of essentially blameless people. His secretary urges him to quit with the words: 'If we lost our jobs, we'd feel like a pair of pants that have been disinfected.' To which Robinson replies: 'Ideals won't put a patch on your pants.' Confronted by the daughter of a woman who killed herself rather than face further humiliation by headline, Robinson snatches for the newsman's standard defence against the charge of amorality. 'Newspapers,' he says, 'are only great mirrors that reflect the world.'

In the 1970s, Hollywood's mirror briefly reflected a more positive image of newsroom life. *All the President's Men* (1976), starring Robert Redford and Dustin Hoffman, delivered a gripping account of the story of the decade: the *Washington Post*'s exposure of the Watergate conspiracy. Soon, Jane Fonda was exposing nuclear skulduggery in *The China Syndrome* (1979) and Clark Kent, *Daily Planet* reporter turned Superman, made his own transition from comic book to cinema screen. But the mood didn't last. Films like *Broadcast News* (1987) have shown

16. The burglary on the offices of the Democratic Party's Watergate offices in 1972 led to the downfall of President Richard Nixon. It also initiated the most famous newspaper investigation of all time and a golden era of investigative reporting. The two reporters, Carl Bernstein and Bob Woodward of the *Washington Post*, were played in the subsequent Hollywood film by Dustin Hoffman and Robert Redford. Since then, every political scandal is labelled 'something-Gate'.

17. The heroic age of journalism, when newspapermen set the world to rights, is nowhere better captured than in the comic-strip stories of Clark Kent, *Daily Planet* reporter, who turns into Superman to combat global evil.

journalistic integrity taking second place to glamour and entertainment. *The Insider* (1998) portrayed a television journalism corrupted by corporate self-interest and in *To Die For* (2000), Nicole Kidman plays a young woman willing to corrupt schoolchildren and murder her husband in order to get a break in TV news documentaries.

Journalism Kills

If Hollywood's journalists are ethically challenged, so they are too in real life. On 15 October 1978, Rupert Murdoch's *News of the World* published a story about a maths teacher, Arnold Lewis, who organized sex parties for consenting adults in his caravan in the Welsh hills. In between the time when the undercover reporters phoned to inform him of his impending notoriety and press time, Lewis gassed himself in his car. At the inquest, the female reporter whose byline appeared on the story was asked by the coroner whether the contents of Lewis's suicide note upset her. 'No, not really,' she replied. Many years later, her editor confessed that the incident still kept him awake at night.[3]

Ethics Mocked

Do journalists take ethics seriously? There are many reasons to think they do not. One of the most widely used text books in the training of British journalists introduces the subject of ethics with the following words:

> To the outsider, journalism and ethics are about as incongruous a mixture as you can get. Even to put the two words in the same sentence is to risk reducing the listener to helpless laughter. To the insider on a mass-market tabloid, ethics are largely an irrelevance. Editors, pressured by intense competition for readers, demand that staff cut ethical corners; and competition among staff encourages some to respond. Lecturing these journalists about ethics is as pointless as advocating celibacy to sailors arriving in port after six months at sea.[4]

Or, as Kelvin Mackenzie, legendary editor of the British tabloid, the *Sun* during the 1980s, once put it: 'Ethics is a place to the east of London where the men wear white socks.'

No wonder that *Private Eye*, the satirical magazine that specializes in poking fun at the media, locates the newspaper industry in 'the Street of Shame', where its spineless hacks, like Lunchtime O'Booze, do the bidding of an absurd proprietor, Lord Gnome, who functions with the lawyers (Sue, Grabbit, and Runne) at one elbow and his curvaceous assistant, Ms Rita Chevrolet, at the other.

Piety at the Post

There is greater piety elsewhere. The *Washington Post Desk-book on Style*[5] reiterates the principles laid down when Eugene Meyer bought the paper in 1933. It begins: 'The first mission of a newspaper is to tell the truth as nearly as the truth may be ascertained.' Among its other solemn pronouncements is the following:

> The newspaper's duty is to its readers and to the public at large, and not to the private interests of the owner. In the pursuit of truth, the newspaper shall be prepared to make sacrifices of its material fortunes, if such course be necessary for the public good. The newspaper shall not be the ally of any special interest, but shall be fair and free and wholesome in its outlook on public affairs and public men.

The *Post*'s manual, which like all newspaper style books also lays out rules on spelling and the differences in word usage, such as theater and theatre, runs to more than 200 pages. Yet, according to one study, the verbosity of what in many news organizations is referred to as the 'bible' cannot conceal some rather glaring omissions. Of thirty-three American newspaper manuals analysed by the Poynter Institute in 1999, the length ranged from 500 to 8,000 words, the favoured subjects for rule-making concerned conflicts of interest, politics, and the acceptance of gifts and junkets.

Missing from many codes were standards or discussion of privacy, deception, identification of juvenile suspects and racial stereotyping. Fewer than one in five codes addressed the subject of editorial and advertising department tensions. Many codes ignored the subject of enforcement.[6]

The BBC and the PCC

In Britain, the BBC's guidelines for producers are even longer, taking in rules on everything from impartiality (which is required by law in the case of all licensed UK broadcasters), fairness, privacy, taste and decency, violence, the depiction of children on television, conflicts of interest, and much else. The *Editor's Code of Practice*,[7] upon which the British Press Complaints Commission bases its adjudication of complaints against newspapers, is a four-page document that gives a good indication of the central ethical standards which journalists in many parts of the world regard as ethically relevant. These are:

- Accuracy, and the prompt correction of inaccuracies.
- The opportunity to reply to attack or criticism.
- Prohibition of invasion of privacy, including by long-lens cameras, except in cases involving genuine public interest.
- Harassment is forbidden, except in cases of public interest.

- Intrusion upon people suffering grief or shock must be 'made with sympathy and discretion.'
- Children should not be bothered at school, or interviewed or photographed without parental consent under the age of 16.
- No use of listening devices, or phone-tapping, except in cases of public interest.
- Hospitals: journalists should not operate covertly.
- Misrepresentation: 'Journalists must not generally seek to obtain information or pictures through misrepresentation or subterfuge.' Such information 'should be removed only with the consent of the owner'. Again, there is a public interest.
- An individual's race, gender, religion, sexual orientation, or disability is only to be mentioned in stories where directly relevant.
- Financial journalism: no use for personal profit of information received; no writing about shares in which a journalist has an interest, without permission of the editor.
- Confidentiality of sources must be protected. This is 'a moral obligation'.
- Payment for stories is acceptable, but not where payment is made to criminals or their associates. Again, there is a public interest test.

The case of the Press Complaints Commission is important, not least because its approach has been much emulated in recent years within emerging democracies in the Balkans, Asia, Africa, and elsewhere. The PCC has also played a key role in developing a global network of self-regulatory press bodies around the Alliance of Independent Press Councils of Europe. These initiatives are not to be confused with the World Association of Press Councils, a body accused by its European enemies of providing a front for state-dominated media organizations, intent upon a censorious global code of ethics for journalists reminiscent of the 'world information order' promoted in the 1980s by UNESCO.

Viewed from this perspective, the PCC is nobly upholding the liberal traditions of the country which pioneered press freedom. Viewed from another, it is 'a somnolent body', which 'emerges sometimes, but only to defend the privacy of Britain's royal families, the Windsors and the Blairs',[8] and which is 'designed largely to keep the newspaper industry out of trouble with politicians, who have in the last two decades repeatedly threatened to legislate to protect citizens against atrocious behaviour by journalists, especially newspapers journalists.'

The case against the PCC is that its rhetoric is strong, but its powers weak. Its only sanction is to oblige newspapers to publish its adjudications and its influence has certainly not prevented newspapers, on a daily basis, declining to make prompt corrections, publishing inaccurate stories, or frequently violating almost every other item in the code. Because so many of its rules may be broken on grounds of 'public interest' (defined as anything which exposes crime, protects public safety, or prevents the public being misled) rules which appear very strong are in practice rather negotiable.

So, for example, the rule which forbids payments to criminals or their associates, did not prevent the PCC from condoning the *Sun*'s decision in 2001 to pay large sums to the agents and family of Ronnie Biggs, an ageing escaped convict flown back to Britain from Brazil by the newspaper amid great scenes of self-congratulation. The editor of the *Mirror*, found guilty of multiple breaches of the code on share dealing in the same year, merely published the adjudication and carried on editing. When a television newsreader, Anna Ford, protested at the secret photographs taken of her and her children on a foreign beach holiday, her complaint was waved away by the *Daily Mail*, that published the pictures, and by the PCC. Ford branded the PCC 'hopeless', took the matter to court, and lost.[9] These days, it is routine for newspapers to pay for information (a practice once known, disapprovingly as 'cheque-book journalism'), with the result that many stories arise purely from this motivation, commonly when a young woman, sometimes a professional sex worker, is paid to divulge her account of an evening with some hapless celebrity. In 2002 the British government announced that it would take steps to outlaw the payment of money by the news media to witnesses in trials, which also provoked an expression of outrage at this latest violation of 'press freedom'.

The conclusion of the PCC's sympathetic historian, Richard Shannon, is that

> a wide segment of public opinion will never be satisfied with a press self-regulatory regime without powers to punish or to suppress. The industry will never voluntarily pay for such a self-regulatory regime; and any alternative will have to be some arrangement of statutory imposition, which the politicians have made clear they are unwilling to undertake. The result is a comprehensive impasse. Logic is defied, but the system works. It is within the protective embrace of that impasse like a hugely plump duvet, that the PCC survives all hazards, confounds all critics, and lives.[10]

Self-Censorship and Other Crimes

In the United States, there is no such duvet. Individual newspapers or newspaper groups deal with complaints directly and many have 'readers' editors' or ombudsmen with specific powers to consider complaints and seek correction, right of reply, or other form of adjudication. This practice has, in recent years, started to spread into British newspapers as well, where some see it as an emerging self-regulatory tier which will in time encourage the PCC to take a tougher stance against serious misbehaviour.

American journalism, however, also faces serious ethical challenges. According to a survey of nearly 300 journalists in 2000, self-censorship in news is commonplace, much of it resulting from journalists bending to pressure from financial sponsors or advertisers—a problem especially acute in local media. More than a third said that 'news which would hurt the financial interests of a new organization goes unreported'.[11] A previous survey, in 1999, showed that journalists increasingly feel that their work is less accurate, that 'the lines have blurred between commentary and reporting', and that 'pressure to make a profit is hurting the quality of coverage'. Half of the journalists questioned thought that their credibility with the public was a major issue, a point underpinned in surveys of the American public, which show a sharp decline in respect for the news media since the 1980s.[12]

It was to combat this perceived decline in standards and public respect that the Committee of Concerned Journalists came together in 1997, launching its Project for Excellence in Journalism. The project has uncovered data which suggest that only 21 per cent of Americans think the press cares about people, down from 41 per cent fourteen years earlier, and that less than half think the press protects democracy,[13] though this number took a brief upward turn following the events of 11 September 2001. Thirty-eight per cent believed news organizations to be actually 'immoral.'[14]

United they Stand

But the same research also discovered that journalists are surprisingly united in their values, especially in their belief that journalism's central purpose is to hold power to account and to provide the resources of information and opinion upon which democracy thrives. 'News professionals at every level . . . express an adamant allegiance to a set of core standards that are striking in their commonality and in their linkage to the public information mission,' concludes one piece of research. On the other hand, the project also confirmed a growing sense of conflict between the goals of the businesses which own the news media and these civic principles. So, although 'every mission statement on file with the American Society of Newspaper Editors names advancing self-government as the primary goal of the news organization,'[15] corporate lawyers 'advised news companies against codifying their principles in writing for fear that they would be used against them in court'.[16]

A Code from Concern County

Bill Kovach and Tom Rosenstiel, leading figures in this movement for more traditional standards of journalism, have worked up from this research a set of nine principles which are more general in character than the codifications of the PCC, or the detail of broadcaster guidelines, but which seek to identify the characteristics they believe the news media must adopt if they are to be trusted and fulfil their democratic mission. Here is the list[17] in full:

- Journalism's first obligation is to the truth.
- Its first loyalty is to citizens.
- Its essence is a discipline of verification.
- Its practitioners must maintain independence from those they cover.
- It must serve as an independent monitor of power.
- It must provide a forum for public criticism and compromise.
- It must strive to make the significant interesting and relevant.
- It must keep the news comprehensive and proportional.
- Its practitioners must be allowed to exercise their personal conscience.

New News isn't So Sure

This, any first-year media studies student could tell you, is a rather old-fashioned list. Kovach and Rosenstiel acknowledge in their own manifesto that 'the truth' is no longer, if it ever was, uncontested. (A very long time ago, Pontius Pilate asked: 'what is truth?') Critics of the Concerned Journalists have dubbed them barnacle-encrusted defenders of 'Old News', insisting that in a world of easy-access multimedia, there is today a 'New News', interactive and subject to interrogation, engaging the emotions and the spirit as much as the brain, and therefore not bound by the old empirical conventions. In 1992, Jon Katz, the journalist and cultural critic, proclaimed in the pages of *Rolling Stone*:

> In place of the Old News, something dramatic is evolving, a new culture of information, a hybrid New News—dazzling, adolescent, irresponsible, fearless, frightening and powerful. The New News is a heady concoction, part Hollywood film and TV movie, part pop music and pop art, mixed with popular culture and celebrity magazines, tabloid telecasts, cable and home video.[18]

The Concerned Journalists of middle-aged America shudder at this apostasy. 'We understand truth as a goal—at best elusive—and still embrace it,' reply Kovach and Rosenstiel. This unalterable goal is, they say, endangered by many changes in journalism: its speed, the anything-goes spirit of the internet, and the need for journalism to to exaggerate in order to stand out. This is 'creating a new journalism of assertion, which is overwhelming the old journalism of verification'. Traditional skills supporting verification, such as shorthand and the law, are also being neglected.

Should Journalists be Accountable?

To the non-American outsider, the vigour of this debate looks like a promising self-defence mechanism against the complacency of the old journalism and the less desirable aspects of the new. In the United States, wealthy foundations like the Pew Centre for the People and the Press, a backer of the Project for Excellence in Journalism, ensures that there is a quality of data about American journalism which simply does not exist anywhere else and journals like the *Columbia Journalism Review* and the *American Journalism Review* feed a culture of reflection. In the 1990s, the publisher Stephen Brill launched a commercial magazine, *Brill's Content*, dedicated to reporting on news media issues. Although this publication infuriated its enemies with its preppy, self-righteous tone, it chased reporters and editors about the way they did things. *Brill's* also fought for a principle of accountability among journalists: 'who should hold themselves as accountable as any of the subjects they write about.' This extended to the argument that journalists should register their financial and other interests, in the manner now customarily expected of elected politicians. Sadly, *Brill's Content* was a fatality when media revenues turned downwards in the first years of the new century.

In Britain, which has neither a *Brill's Content* nor a *Columbia Journalism Review*, there is a low rumble of assent to some of these ideas, usually without much in the way of comprehensive evidence. 'Print journalism is now the most corrupt realm of life in Britain,' wrote one national newspaper journalist in 2002. 'Some journalists boast of lifestyles that are little more than perpetual junkets—bribes—from those whose news they report.'[19] Or to cite an earlier clarion call: 'The business is now subject to a contagious outbreak of squalid, banal, lazy and cowardly journalism whose only qualification is that it helps to make newspaper publishers (and some journalists) rich.'[20] In Britain, however, the well-tried principle that dog shall not eat dog in the news media persists, explaining why in 2002, the owners of the *Daily Mail* and *Daily Express*, deadly commercial rivals, quietly acceded to the suggestion that they should cease attacking each others' owners.

This statute of limitations, however, does not inhibit one country's journalists from pontificating about another's. France, for instance, unlike Britain, affords legal privacy protection to public figures and is, as a result, often castigated for lily-livered journalism by true-blooded Anglo-Saxon scribes. Here, for example, is a British commentary on the French presidential election in 2002.

> What's striking is how utterly toothless the French TV interviewers are in the face of these two men's dual campaign banalathons, how repellently deferential. . . . When Chirac was cross-examined by Poivre d'Arvor on TF1 recently, it was like watching an old man being gummed by a toothless spaniel . . . His showpiece July 14 interview with the president last year allowed the oleaginous incumbent, embroiled in a range of corruption scandals that would have destroyed the political careers of British politicians five times over, to slide away unscathed. . . . As one foreign journalist argued this week, the British press would have hounded such a man out of politics years ago.'[21]

A Philosopher Intervenes

Not everyone, however, is content with the British press's assessment of its own standards. In her Reith lectures of 2002, a prestigious event which commemorates the founding director general of the BBC, the Oxford phlilosopher Onora O'Neill took the theme of trust. In her final lecture, she turned to the press which, she said, was guilty of 'smears, sneers and jeers, names, shames and blames. Some reporting covers (or should I say "uncovers") dementing amounts of trivia, some misrepresents, some denigrates, some teeters on the brink of defamation . . . If the media mislead, or if readers cannot assess their reporting, the wells of public discourse and public life are poisoned.'

Onora O'Neill is surely right that the ethic of truthfulness and accuracy is at the heart of the morality of journalism, even if one accepts that neither quality is capable of incontestable definition. Without these qualities, journalism cannot inspire trust and without trust, there is no worthwhile journalism. Industry codes and the law of the land both have a part to play in framing and policing the necessary standards, but as we have seen in the financial services industry, which is regulated in minute detail, dishonesty among auditors and senior managers still goes undetected. That is one reason why Kovach and Rosenstiel are right, in their ninth and final article of faith, to turn to the conscience of the individual journalist.

Working with young, would-be journalists in a journalism school, I encountered real and justified nervousness about what these people will be expected to do, in order to prove themselves as fearless and effective reporters. Veterans of the business tell hugely entertaining stories about the stunts and deceptions they have engaged in to throw a rival reporter off the scent, or keep a prize witness to themselves. But where should the line be drawn? Is it all right to apply emotional pressure to a parent who has lost a child in tragic circumstances to hand over a treasured picture? Is it OK, as Hildy Johnson suggests, to steal the photo from the mantlepiece? What about stealing a document, or a glance at a document when your interviewee is momentarily distracted, or called from the room? In what circumstances would you lie to get a bigger truth? Would you ever be prepared to disguise or conceal your identity? It depends, doesn't it? It would be acceptable to most people to pose as the purchaser of a dodgy car in order to expose a dealer whose business is in selling dodgy cars. But to pose as a doctor, in order to get someone to tell you their intimate health concerns, would be another matter. In these sorts of cases, code books only get you so far and, in any case, what is forbidden in one news organization may be regarded as a matter for celebration in another. How else to make sense of a professional world which extends from the *Washington Post*'s rule that 'in gathering news, reporters will not misrepresent their identity. They will not identify themselves as police officers, physicians or anything other than journalists'[22] to custom and practice on the *News of the World*, London's biggest selling newspaper, whose most famous investigative reporter habitually dresses up in robes and pretends to be a sheikh in order to entrap his victims?

This is My Truth, Tell Me Yours

So when journalism students ask me how they should navigate through a world of such contrasts, where the captain of every ship speaks a different language, it is difficult to make any other reply than this. Journalists are part of the societies in which they work. They acquire, within those societies, a sense of right and wrong; they have, thank goodness, a moral compass learnt outside journalism. It is up to every individual to preserve that compass, to be true to their own and their community's values. In short, don't expect your employer, or the news industry, to do it for you.

Who are These Journalists Anyway?

This conclusion leads, inevitably, to the question of who the journalists are. Where do they come from? What makes them tick? What do they believe in?

These questions are not so easily answered as may be imagined since there is no very clear agreement on how to define a journalist. Does the definition include news presenters, who may be actors rather than people trained in news? Does it include radio talk-show and tabloid TV hosts; does it include someone who sets up a weblog on the internet and shares information and opinion with anyone willing to pay attention? What about researchers on a television documentary, or researchers on an entertaining quiz based on the news? Or take the astrology column in a newspaper, which may sit alongside a readers' letters feature: are either of these the work of a journalist, or both? Is there a common set of standards to which both might be expected to work?

In Britain, even the number of journalists is subject to a wide range of estimates. Some put the figure as low as 15,000, others as high as 120,000, though the best guess is probably in the 60,000 to 70,000 range. Thanks to a recent, and rare, piece of research, we do have a reasonably up-to-date portrait of the British working journalist.[23] The essential characteristics of contemporary British journalists are:

- as likely to be a woman as a man;
- young: 70 per cent of journalists are under 40;
- childless: only 23 per cent have dependent children;
- white: only 4 per cent are from ethnic minority groups
- metropolitan: 55 per cent work in London and the South East;
- middle-class: only 3 per cent of new entrants have parents who are unskilled or semi-skilled;
- graduates (98 per cent);
- low-paid: the average salary is £22,500, though stars earn more than ten times that level.

It is difficult to make comparisons across national boundaries, though we do know that ensuring that journalism reflects the ethnic diversity of the populations it serves is proving a struggle in many places. The British ethnic minority figure of 4 per cent compares with a national figure of over 10 per cent of ethnic minority people in the population as a whole, and a figure much higher than that in the urban centres where most journalists work. In the United States, minorities account for 30 per cent of the population, but fewer than 12 per cent of newspaper journalists.[24]

The Global Journalist

Professor David Weaver of Indiana University has worked for a number of years with a group of academics around the world, attempting to throw light upon facts about journalists. His most recent research,[25] which covers twenty-one countries, suggests the following:

- Journalism is still a predominantly male occupation, though it is becoming less so. New Zealand and Finland are among the countries that achieved gender balance first.
- Journalists are young, on average in their mid-30s, which is younger than the workforce average.
- They come overwhelmingly and disproportionately from the dominant ethnic group in their societies. This is a

serious problem almost everywhere, but especially so in Britain, the United States, Taiwan, and Canada and to a lesser degree in Brazil and China.

- They are increasingly, and in some countries almost universally, university-educated, though the extent to which they bother with 'journalism schools' or 'journalism degrees' varies hugely.

What do Journalists Believe?

An even more interesting, and largely unexplored question, is: what do these journalists believe? What is their ethical framework? The researchers found that most journalists agree they are in the business of getting information to the public quickly, but there are wide differences of view about the extent to which journalists do or should see themselves as 'watchdogs' on government or other centres of power. This is a highly rated objective among journalists in Australia, Britain, and Finland, but much less so in countries which lack a long history of democratic government and a culture of a free press. Algeria, Taiwan, and Chile provide examples among the countries surveyed.

Nor could journalists really agree on the importance of their role as analysts, or whether they have an obligation to report accurately or objectively. Only 30 per cent of a British sample agreed that journalists are obliged to be accurate and objective.

In Germany, over 80 per cent of journalists, and in the US 49 per cent, accept this obligation. German journalists, who are regarded by their British counterparts as rather dull and cautious creatures, say they are much less happy about harassing sources, using documents without permission, and paying for information. Impersonation is frowned upon more by journalists in Australia than those of other countries. A rare point of (near) agreement is that all around the world (Finland is recorded as an exception) journalists think it unacceptable to be forced to divulge the sources of their information. Perhaps the Finns take the view that a journalist's social responsibility to cooperate with law enforcement exceeds the imperative of the confidentiality principle. In 2002, a group of British newspapers found themselves retesting this issue the hard way, when they were ordered by the courts and the London financial markets regulator, the FSA, to hand over a leaked, but erroneous bid document involving a company called Interbrew. Where did the balance of justice lie here? In the regulator's responsibility to see plain dealing in financial markets or the journalist's protection of the sender of the unmarked brown envelope?

Journalists are Lefties

The British work for the Weaver survey was carried out by Tony Delano and John Henningham. They add one very interesting point of information about British journalists. Interviewed in 1995, and therefore at the spluttering near-expiry of sixteen years of Conservative government, only 6 per cent of journalists questioned said they would vote Conservative at the next election and 57 per cent expressed support for Labour. The journalists, it is reported, 'generally took liberal positions on a range of social, economic and moral issues',[26] which tends to confirm a widely held assumption that journalists are mostly of a leftish or liberal disposition. This is certainly the view held by the American public.[27]

Back to the Conscience Clause

It is perhaps not surprising, in the light of findings such as these, that there is confusion about standards of behaviour in journalism. There simply is no lingua franca of journalistic ethics. Journalism is an occupation, especially in newspapers and magazines, which prides itself upon the absence of regulation and which, by its very nature, is simultaneously trying both to tune into and challenge the moral and political reflexes of the societies in which it functions. If journalism is, in its origin and purpose, concerned with the expression and testing of public opinion in all its diversity, we should not be surprised that it lacks a tightly disciplined rule-book. It remains to be seen whether convergence of print and audio-visual media via the internet and other digital platforms will result in regulation of the press becoming more like broadcasting or vice versa. What is certain, however, is that we will not achieve high moral standards in journalism by accident. Journalists, expert at putting others under pressure, need to be under pressure themselves. The rest of the world can learn a lot from the American example of collecting accurate data about journalists and the the public's view of them. Information, good journalism if you like, is the key to the debate on media ethics, as to so much else. Healthy democracies need transparent data about communications and communicators, so that they can debate the business of journalism with authority and insight.

7

Matt's Modem

Tomorrow's Journalism

For a couple of years at the end of the 1990s, the world of journalism went crazy. It was impossible to be among journalists without hearing of someone who was leaving their job to set up a web-based news service or an e-zine, to work for Microsoft or Yahoo, or to develop their existing employers' burgeoning on-line services. A friend of mine not only left his newspaper to make his fortune on the web, he also invested his pension money in technology, media, and communication stocks. There were so many jobs, it became difficult to recruit people into journalism training courses. Who needs training when there are jobs galore for anyone with enthusiasm and a bit of dotcom attitude?

It was a time when everyone thought they needed to be in everyone else's business. Newspapers were terrified that the internet would steal their readers and their classified advertising, so they even started creating websites for advertisers to try to keep them loyal. Magazines rushed to create new identities on-line and in multi-channel television. Television piled into interactive services, to head off the internet challenge. And just about everyone thought about merging, to deal with the much proclaimed 'convergence' of the computer, telecommunications, television, and newspaper industries via the new digital technology.

Some gambled billions on these schemes. Others merely doubled the size of their editorial staffs. Newspaper editors wrote of their 'e-epiphanies', as they finally understood that the internet would transform the media. 'What the hell were we all smoking that weekend?' is the question now asked at Time Warner, according to Rupert Murdoch,[1] reflecting upon the decision by Time Warner to sell itself into a merger with America Online at the very peak of dotcom valuations, with the result that it inflicted huge, medium-term misery on its own shareholders. Never in the history of journalism has a new medium appeared so rapidly out of the blackness and with such volatile consequences. This was journalism on cocaine: the New New Thing meets Woodward and Bernstein. Now the party is over, we still need to figure out what the internet and other new news mean for tomorrow's journalism. And how important are these technological issues, against the other concerns discussed in this book, about journalistic ethics and ownership and the central question of the freedom to publish?

Hacks and Hackers

My own experience with the internet began very badly, with the net surfacing as an accessory to the worst mistake I ever made as a journalist. It was the autumn of 1994 and I had been for a few months editor of the *Independent*, a British daily newspaper born as an independent voice outside the club of traditional newspaper owners eight years earlier. When I took over, the paper was in a mess. Circulation had fallen from a peak of 400,000 to 250,000; Rupert Murdoch had started a price war against us; our equipment was worn out and the founders had been forced to surrender their independence to a group of large European publishers, who handed management control to the Mirror Group, which was itself still recovering from the aftermath of a scandalous period when its pensioners were defrauded by the paper's owner, Robert Maxwell.

There was a lot to do. The paper needed redesigning for the *Mirror*'s presses, the editorial budget was slashed, and we moved to offices alongside the *Mirror*, high in London's biggest office block at Canary Wharf, determined to start rebuilding sales. We also needed to break news, something for which the *Independent* had never been noted. One day, in late 1994, David Felton, the paper's news editor, whispered to me that we were on to a big story. He had been in touch with a young freelance reporter, based in Scotland, who claimed to have hacked into the computer system of BT, the national telephone company, and gained access to all secret telephone numbers in the UK. Among these were direct lines to the most protected defence and intelligence establishments and the prime minister's flat in Downing Street.

It obviously needed a lot of checking. We made enquiries about the reporter, who was in touch with a known network of investigative journalists. He showed us lengthy print-outs of the telephone numbers. We tested them and they were accurate. He said that he had transferred the electronic version of the files to an undisclosed location on the internet. Eventually, we put the allegations to BT, which said its data was totally secure. We published the story on the front page of the paper and it caused a stir. The prime minister was asked about it in the House of Commons. BT continued to insist that its system was sound. A police investigation was launched. We took calls from BT staff contradicting the official BT line: the system was anything but secure, they told us, and this could be proved a second time, if we would make a reporter available.

By now, I was starting to have doubts. A former colleague from the *Financial Times*, a computer expert, in days when the internet was not a widely understood phenomenon, said the description we had published of the use made by hackers of the internet simply did not make sense. Our freelance stood by his account, but could no longer produce the electronic version of his secret data, which he now said he had obliterated to cover his traces. We brought in an expert to comb the hard drive of his computer. We could not find the data. I suggested that the freelancer spend a few hours at my flat in further conversation with Felton and the senior reporter with whom he had worked on the story. By midnight, we had a confession. The data had been secured not by hackers or gum-shoe journalism, but downloaded from a computer when the reporter worked at BT, on a temporary contract arranged by an employment agency. He had not wished to tell us this, because he thought he would get into trouble. He wanted to make a name for himself as a journalist.

Meanwhile, another *Independent* reporter, John Arlidge, was already checking out the calls we had taken from inside BT, appearing to corroborate security lapses. One source was a trade union official in North East England, who offered to demonstrate that our reporter could walk straight past BT's security, sit down at a computer, log on and inspect the secret telephone numbers detailed in our report. This is exactly what subsequently happened and, as our 'hacker's' story fell apart, we reported the results to our readers. Soon, Arlidge and the BT official were prosecuted under a new law to protect computer data. We learnt that we had won this case a year later, ironically the day after I was sacked as editor of the paper, following my refusal to implement a second round of cuts in the newsroom. The press release issued by the company thanked me for my services, noted that circulation had risen to 290,000, but said the paper needed a new editor to take it to the next stage. Within a year, it was struggling to sell 200,000 copies a day, a position from which it has not recovered.

The initial shame I felt about the story was simply that we had failed to check it out adequately: we should have been more sceptical about our freelance contact. I was also angry that a perfectly good story—BT secret data at risk because of slack supervision of contractors—had been destroyed by a bogus one about hacking. In essence, the two stories raised the same public issue, but the internet had been used to give the story glamour, and as a cover for its originator. The years have intensified rather than diminished my embarrassment because like everyone else I can now see that the way we portrayed the internet in 1994 was deeply ignorant. The idea that the internet, the most public medium in the history of communication, would be used as a hiding place for a hacker's secret data was a bit like suggesting a gang of bank robbers might choose to hide a sack of stolen bullion on the bar of an East End pub.

The Meaning of the Internet

So, what does the internet, along with other new digital communications technologies such as interactive television, mean for journalism? Some things are clear. Digital offers a huge expansion in the amount of data which can be forced through any communications network, and allows it to be manipulated and displayed upon a range of cheap and simple desk-top, hand-held, or living-room devices. Since the telecommunications network is global, leaving aside issues of communications poverty in large tracts of the world, journalism has become, almost at a stroke, a global enterprise.

For professional journalists, this has very big implications. The global nature of the new communications network means that individuals can consume journalism made all over the world, and discuss it, interactively, across national boundaries. Journalism today is a two-way street, or rather a multidirectional process in a boundaryless space, rather than the one-way street of the traditional newspaper or television news bulletin. Also, because the technology of news-making and distribution is much cheaper and simpler, even in the previously highly protected areas of television and radio, it means that almost anyone can join in the journalistic mêlée. Today's newsrooms are, essentially, collections of networked personal computers. Some of today's mobile phones can record and transmit pictures, sound, and text, turning them into primitive television stations. The interplay between mobile phone traffic, live television, and other news media around the 11 September terrorist attacks on America provided one compelling illustration of the way that contemporary political struggles are correctly seen as, in one sense, phenomena involving both private and public media.

It is not, in my opinion, an exaggeration to use the word 'revolution' to describe changes as far-reaching as these, none of which are rendered void by the switch-back motions of the stock market and the valuation of technology, media, and communication stocks. These markets will still play an important role in determining the speed and extent to which truly high-speed broadband communications networks will be rolled out, but nothing the markets can now do will turn this revolution around.

What we have already witnessed since the early 1990s is remarkable enough. It is now routine for consumers to receive 200 or 300 television channels, rather than three or four. Radio, rather than being squashed by television, has also entered a new and dramatic growth phase. In the pre-digital era of the 1990s, Britain went from under 50 to 250 commercial radio stations. Digital radio will increase that by an unknowable factor. Newspapers, although under pressure for share of advertising markets and reader time, are today able to print at low cost in multiple sites, rather than moving vast quantities of newsprint by road or rail over large distances. They too encounter global possibilities. Magazine titles, supremely well-suited to targeting niche markets, have also continued to multiply. In terms of the news business, magazines play a relatively small part in people's lives, in the sense of their priority as a straight news medium, but today no other medium is able to reach so effectively across the whole social-demographic spectrum as magazines.[2] Magazines not only serve highly specialized markets in business and among hobbyists; they have also been responsible for significant extensions of cultural identity among women, young people, and ethnic minorities. Think only of, say, the influence of a magazine like *Cosmopolitan* upon the lifestyle of women in Western countries in the 1970s and 1980s.

In television, satellite communications and digital editing make it possible for reporters to transmit stories more or less from anywhere to anywhere, and for editors to process them rapidly for broadcast or World Wide Web outlets. Lightweight cameras and other equipment, combined with modern air travel, makes it possible for television journalists to be on the scene of stories in hours, where once it would have involved days. To me, it only seems like yesterday that on many foreign assignments the most difficult part of the job was the length of the queue at the local telex station, to transmit a simple message back to head office. Working as an editor in a national newspaper office, the most irksome aspect of the job up until the 1980s was negotiating with printers, whose baroque trade union structures placed layers of difficulty between the journalist and the printed page. Today, journalists seldom meet printers. News is multimedia, instant, global, and ubiquitous.

Drudge and the Kids from Fame

As for the internet itself, it has already caused an enormous stir as a medium of news. The most controversial figure, to date, is the patron saint (or, in the eyes of many journalists, patron sinner) of on-line journalism, Matt Drudge, the Hollywood-based, one-man-band reporter who started out doing star gossip and movie ratings, but in January 1998 had the American news media at his feet, when he learned that *Newsweek Magazine*, owned by the Washington Post group, had held back from publishing an account of President Clinton's sexual liaison with a White House intern, Monica Lewinsky. Drudge, who had been following the rumours about Clinton's sexual activities for some time, got confirmation of the story from a New York literary agent, wrote his report, and dispatched it to his readers. Although it is very likely that this story would have surfaced somewhere without Drudge, the scoop became a point of definition in American journalism, the Watergate of its day, when it precipitated a scramble for angles on the same story by established newspaper and television reporters, in which corners were cut, mistakes made, and rumours paraded as fact. The final irony was that when the official investigation into the Lewinsky affair was published, it was the first such official report to be made instantly available on the internet, causing news sites around the world to freeze under the burden of traffic. To 'new news' people, this was a revolutionary triumph. To traditionalists, it was American journalism's darkest hour. According to polls at the time, the news media's behaviour inflamed public opinion not against the president, but against the news media. President Clinton survived impeachment and would probably have won re-election to the White House in 2000, had he not reached the extent of his term limit.

It is worth recapturing, in Drudge's own words, the composition of that momentous Drudge Report of 9.02 p.m., Pacific Time, 17 January 1998:

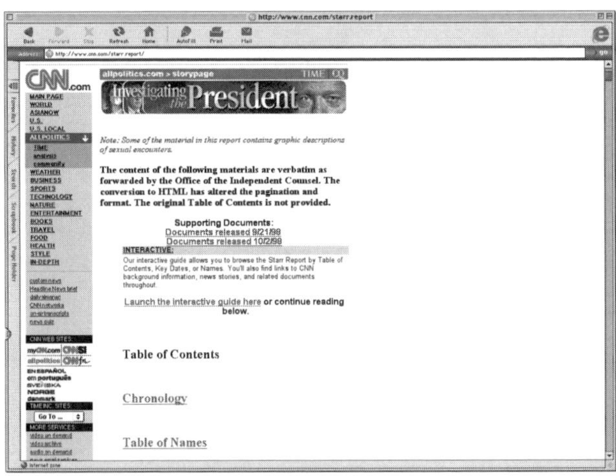

18. Internet first! When the Starr Report into the allegations against President Bill Clinton, concerning his relationship with White House intern Monica Lewinsky, was published on the World Wide Web in 1998, it caused systems around the world to crash.

Nothing left to do.

My finger's poised over the button.

This is everything.

Everything you've ever been and everything you'll ever be. . . .

'*Whaddya think yer doin', Drudge? . . .*'

Cat. Bummer.

'*Am I reading this right? You're about to accuse POTUS [the President of the United States] of having it off with an intern? Are you preparing to blow up Washington? Get me Janet Reno . . . !*'

Hey, I don't like it either, but it's confirmed confirmed confirmed, and your Janet Reno's authorized Starr to move in. . . .'

'*You are a terrorist, aren't you?*'

Mommy and Daddy were liberals . . .

'*You and your internet manifesto.*'

Let the future begin.

'*So be it . .* '

Microsoft mouse moved into position.

Ready. Aim. ENTER.

Bouncing beams from dish to dish, e's, faxes & alarms. 1 am

Cellphones, conference calls, dirty dresses, cigars. 2 am

Subpoenas. Grand Juries. Fallout. 3 am.

Elections. Impeachment. 4 am

Acquittal 5 am.

Fame 6 am

Dawn.[3]

Note the penultimate line. Fame: Drudge, the ingenue, knew perfectly well that he was playing for media celebrity. Six months later, he was the guest of the National Press Club in Washington. During his remarks, he spoke idealistically of 'an era vibrating with the din of small voices'. He went on: 'Every citizen can be a reporter, can take on the powers that be. The difference between the internet, television and radio, magazines, newspapers is the two-way communication. The Net gives as much voice to a 13-year-old computer geek like me as to a CEO or Speaker of the House. We all become equal.'[4]

Drudge wears a trilby hat, like a 1920s muck-raking journalist, and his supporters see him carrying the torch for the journalistic tradition of Tom Paine and Thomas Jefferson. The reaction at the Press Club, however, was not so favourable. Doug Harbrecht, the *Business Week* journalist then serving as Press Club president led the inquisition, and Drudge scratched hard into his shaky knowledge of American news history to defend himself. But his return fire took casualties. The high-speed, rolling, error-prone editions of on-line journalism, he likened to the heyday of the yellow press, when newspapers would turn out a dozen editions a day. If he made mistakes, he said, so did the august news

19. Matt Drudge, cyber-muck-raker, broke the Monica Lewinsky story on his Drudge Report website. When he faced his professional press critics at Washington's National Press Club, he told them: 'I am not a professional journalist. I am not paid by anyone.'

organizations represented in the room. Then he added: 'I put my name on every single thing I write. No "Periscope" here. No "Washington Whispers" there.'[5] Moreover, he said, he was committed to 'cover media people the way they cover politicians . . . How did a story like Monica Lewinsky break out of a Hollywood apartment? What does that say about the Washington press corps?' The media, he said, 'is comparable to government—probably passes government in raw power', so had to be interrogated. As for the rules of journalism, concerning the number of sources needed to establish a reliable fact before publication, Drudge said: 'I follow my conscience . . . conscience is going to be the only thing between us and the communication in the future, now. And I'm very happy with my conscience.' Recall, if you will the final, ninth article in the manifesto of 'old journalism', *The Elements of Journalism*: 'practitioners must be allowed to exercise their personal conscience.'[6]

Harbrecht asked whether Drudge foresaw 'a separation of media practices where future journalists accept more your style and methods, or accept the methods of *appropriate* journalism?' Note the menacing, establishment tone in the word 'appropriate'. The only problem Drudge could see was that, if there were thousands of reporters like him clamouring for attention, 'it could start looking like an insane asylum'. But if that happened, 'I think people will grow disinterested. But again, they'll rally around something else. So I leave this to the free marketplace.' Where, Harbrecht persisted, did this leave the 'professional ethic of journalism'? To which Drudge replied: 'Professional. You see, the thing is you are throwing these words at me that I can't defend, because I am not a professional journalist. I am not paid by anyone.'

By the time you read this book, Matt Drudge may have vanished without a trace, or he may be fronting the most popular talk show on network television. But the issues that his work raises, and the moral hinterland from which he proceeds, are those that have emerged consistently in the themes of this book. The defence of the Western, democratic tradition of newspapers lies in its commitment to free expression and free markets, even where markets tend to excess. It is a free market that finds space for Thomas Paine, William Randolph Hearst, John Wilkes, Bob Guccione, the *New York Times*, Michael Moore, and Matt Drudge. It means that the Supreme Court will defend the publishing rights of *Hustler Magazine*, as well as the *Washington Post*. The nobility of principle involved in Thomas Jefferson's according free newspapers a higher democratic priority than free government survives, albeit in high tension with disgust at some of what freedom allows. It should be remembered that, in his later years, Jefferson himself deplored 'the putrid state into which the newspapers have passed and the malignity, the vulgarity and the mendacious spirit of those who write them'.[7] The unmistakable voice of old news, the establishment, repelled by the new.

Bloggers Unite

But if the excitements of Drudge's work carry positive reverberations of these eighteenth-century struggles, they do not dispel all doubt about the internet's future. In the press, an earlier era marked by the din of small voices soon gave way to an era of larger, industrial voices, competition for advertising, libel laws, and other civil restraints, which held the worst excesses of newspapers in check, while also in some cases suppressing what ought not to have been suppressed. The press then had to come to terms with competition from the oligopolistic world of broadcast news, which it initially feared would lead to the destruction of newspapers. In practice, television differed from print in many significant ways, in terms of the volume and complexity of information each medium could convey, and in terms of its relationship with the state. The internet is, in a sense, the bastard child of both broadcasting and print. Some of the biggest players in on-line journalism are television news companies, such as CNN and the BBC. Other news websites are off-shoots of newspapers. But the internet is also home to Matt Drudge and a galaxy of other small-time operators and newcomers, discharging their news, views, and impressions to anyone prepared to pay attention.

The extent to which the medium will remain hospitable to such anarchic free-booters is difficult to say, but history tells us that no medium of journalism lasts long if it is unsupported by a clear business model and that is where the internet has encountered difficulty. Newspapers, magazines, commercial radio, and most television eventually moved to a model based chiefly upon advertising. But television's diversity has been increased by the availability of subsidy from the taxpayer and today, increasingly, by the emergence of a new revenue stream in subscription-financed channels, programmes, or events. It is interesting to note that the world's highest levels of per capita expenditure on television occur in the United States, which is the largest market, and the United Kingdom, which has in relative terms the largest publicly funded broadcaster.[8]

On-line journalism is still finding its way both financially and creatively. It attracted vast sums of capital in the late 1990s, based largely upon a misunderstanding of the speed with which the internet would transform commercial and personal communication, and has since struggled to establish workable, day-to-day business models. Advertising on the internet is problematic because of the limited size of display screens and the fact that adverts are widely seen as too intrusive in a medium which, unlike television, demands the same level of concentration as reading. But subscription only works for publications with a high 'need to know' element, which is difficult to sustain at a time when news organizations are providing free on-line access to such large amounts of material. Probably the dominant approach currently among on-line news services is for the on-line product to draw almost entirely upon the creative resources of the print or broadcast parent, but to offer users additional, paid-for services, such as access to archive. As 'old media' have started to understand the internet, they have also worked hard to blunt its challenge, by using their own web operations to shore up newspaper classified advertising sales or exploiting their on-line offerings as promotional vehicles for paper-based products, which are still more portable and easily read. This is a good example of Brian Winston's 'law of suppressed radical potential'[9] which works to slow down the incursion of new technology, to the astonishment of techo-utopians of all ages.

The advantages of electronic on-line media, however, will continue to assert themselves, as more people have access to on-line information at higher speeds and lower prices. As computing, communications, and screen technologies advance further, it is very likely that we shall see a disposable floppy 'screen', which can be inscribed with electronic ink via a phone line or wireless link, and stuffed into your pocket or briefcase. Reverses in the markets' view of dotcom companies in the early part of this century should not blind us to the fact that on-line media have sustainable advantages over print in terms of both searchability and interactivity.

On-line media also provide a unique opportunity for journalists to combine still and moving pictures, sound, and text. Here lies a great and as yet barely attempted creative challenge, to develop a way of reporting and informing people which feels fresh, startling, and memorable in the way that it did when newspaper publishers first understood how to use headlines, typography, and layout to make navigation of a newspaper more rewarding, and pictures to make the experience more arresting.

Radio made its mark on journalism by bringing the sound of real events to the listener in the Second World War. Television has transfixed us with images of the moment—the young man waving down a tank in Tiananmen Square, the crumbling World Trade Center towers—and transformed our relationship with political leaders through the evolution of the interview. Television graphics have a unique power to explain. Radio can network conversations across the globe, or within the smallest communities.

So far, web journalism has not led to the birth of anything quite so distinctive. But as Matt Drudge's work illustrates, it has placed the power to shake the mighty in the hands of individuals or small groups: a welcome, if provisional, antidote to media concentration, the hegemony of business values, and the complacency into which all professional groups fall from time to time. The internet has also put into reporters' hands new research tools, sometimes called 'Computer Assisted Reporting',[10] and greatly enhanced the ability of reporters to interrogate public databases, which are slowly becoming more accessible under freedom of information legislation. In purely creative terms too, there are also small flares in the night. The work of organizations like the Centre for Digital Storytelling[11] builds upon traditions of oral history and community journalism and puts the tools of multimedia storytelling and journalism into the hands of ordinary citizens. Dana

Winslow Atchley, who died in 2000, is a noted pioneer in the digital storytellers' mission 'to thrill those who stand and listen with the notion that they too might have a voice.'[12]

Another recent manifestation of possibility is the web-logging movement, or blogging. This, like so much on the internet, was pioneered by an individual and made available to others essentially without charge. It permits anyone to establish a real-time, on-line personal platform, for use as a diary or pulpit to the world. Andrew Sullivan, a well-known British journalist, and a former editor of the American magazine *New Republic*, describes Blogging as 'the first journalistic model that harnesses rather than merely exploits the true democratic nature of the web. It's a new medium finally finding a unique voice. Stay tuned as that voice gets louder and louder.' Sullivan's own weblog has even demonstrated that it is possible to develop an income stream, through a mixture of seeking voluntary donations and 'affiliate advertising', which means that the blogger gets cash if the site user clicks through to an advertiser and buys something. Sullivan also runs a book club, in which he shares views with readers on a current book selection and takes a commission from Amazon, the on-line book retailer, for all books purchased.

This means a writer no longer needs a wealthy proprietor to get his message across to readers. He no longer needs an editor, either. It means a vast amount of drivel will find its way to the web. But it also means that a writer is finally free of the centuries-old need to suck up to various entities to get an audience. The universe of permissible opinions will expand. It's no accident that a good plurality of American bloggers are libertarian or right of centre. With a couple of exceptions the established newspaper market in America is dominated by left-liberal editors and reporters. What the web has done is allow talented writer to bypass this coterie and write directly to an audience. If the Drudge Report pioneered the first revolution of this kind, then bloggers are the vanguard of the second wave.[13]

Life and Death

Activities such as blogging and digital storytelling will acquire even greater potential, as higher speed communications networks take shape. There is certainly good reason to hope that they might help fill the growing gaps in local and community news networks,[14] which have opened up as largely monopoly newspapers have cut their reporting resources and relaxed in the absence of competition. Multimedia, on-line communication is also an essential feature of other news networks, such as those formed by fans in sport and entertainment, as well as in highly specialized fields like science and the law. No professional communicator should doubt the power of the internet in the hands of the curious and determined citizen, as poignantly illustrated in the case of 'Miss B', a 43-year-old British woman who demanded of her doctors that they turn off her life support machinery a year after a catastrophic injury had paralysed her. The case was heard by a judge at the bedside of Miss B, who explained that her trust in the doctors, who refused to switch off her ventilator, had been undermined when she surfed the internet and found 'a tremendous amount of information, not just from professionals, but also from other quadriplegics, who are also ventilated'.[15] Empowered by this information, Miss B was able to make her case and the court decided she should be granted her wish to die.

The vibrating din of small voices also enables other professional communicators, such as public relations experts, to communicate directly with the public, rather than only through the media. At the same time, public relations executives must deal with the fact that new media also allow individuals and campaign groups to mount significant media challenges to much larger opponents. In the 1990s, for example, anyone who searched the World Wide Web for the restaurant company McDonalds would quickly find themselves being offered a direct route to sites run by McDonalds's, many angry critics. So-called 'independent media centres' have also sprung up around the world on the back of demonstrations challenging the values of global, free-market capitalism. These centres[16] see themselves as providing information about events unsullied by the preoccupations of the mainstream media. They have been highly visible during the street protests in Seattle in 1999, Davos in 2000 and 2001 and, for example, in April 2002, when Israeli troops invaded the Palestinian town of Jenin. The response of mainstream public relations experts to these developments has been to invest heavily in web monitoring, in order to maintain a real-time watch for their clients upon chat rooms and other internet-based communications forums. Even the British Royal family uses the web to challenge stories in the newspapers and many companies and other organizations now webcast their own video.

Aux Armes Citoyens! Plurality, Diversity, and Trust!

Just how this competition between a din of small voices and the ever-growing scale of the biggest media companies will shake down is impossible to judge. Those who feel pessimistic about the corporatization of the internet and the predicted loss of its diversity should perhaps take comfort from the difficulties now being endured by the new giants: AOL–Time Warner, Disney, and Vivendi have serious troubles, as they try to make sense of convergence and emerging consumer tastes. Equally, those inclined to optimism should recall that power, in the end, follows money in the media, which is why, even in a media world much more difficult to regulate than previously, there will still be good grounds for taxpayers to invest constructively in better news media. This can be achieved by continuing to support 'public interest' and 'public service' news media, which the market would otherwise squeeze out; by insisting upon tough rules against media concentration and by making sure that access to communications infrastructures is affordable and fair. The last point will be crucial if we are not to experience a damaging 'digital divide', which is already apparent in differences between internet use by poorer people and the more prosperous, not to mention the much larger gaps between rich and poor countries. If the slogan of the French revolutionaries was 'liberty, equality, and fraternity', the slogan of the ongoing communications revolution should be: 'plurality, diversity, and trust.'

The confusion of the times arises from the fact that so many apparently contrary things are happening at the same time: we have blogging and AOL–Time Warner; independent media centres and the rise of the global public relations firm; Matt Drudge and the $50m TV news presenter. To some extent, these phenomena can be explained as reactions to each other, all part of the restless churning of the news media, as they resist confinement by old technologies, old establishments, and old certainties.

Gutenberg Galaxy to Internet Galaxy

According to Manuel Castells, whose great trilogy of books in the 1990s mapped the 'network society,' the unique culture of the internet will preserve it from take over by corporations or emasculation by governments,[17] so long as the net's governance is not dominated by American interests.

> The internet is a particularly malleable technology, susceptible of being deeply modifed by its social practice, and leading to a whole range of potential social outcomes—to be discovered by experience, not proclaimed beforehand. . . .[18] it is the expression of ourselves—through a specific code of communication, which we must understand if we want to change our reality.[19]

Castells has also suggested that

> if convergence takes place one day, it will be when the investment required in setting up broadband capabilities beyond the instrumental uses of the corporate world is justified by a new media system wiling and ready to satisfy the most important latent demand: the demand for interactive free expression and autonomous creation—nowadays largely stymied by the sclerotic vision of the traditional media industry.[20]

Journalism is self-evidently only an aspect of this larger media picture, yet there is no denying that it will both shape and be shaped by the forces Castells identifies. The combination of social, political, technological, and economic circumstances which gave us the liberal free press settlement in the eighteenth century no longer exists in the same form today. As we navigate our way from Marshall McLuhan's 'Gutenberg Galaxy' to the Castells' 'Internet Galaxy', the great driving force is the citizen-consumer, who today demands maximum choice and maximum quality; who wishes to be both frivolous and serious; to flit from one medium of news to another, and to pick up news when the mood strikes, no longer feeling obliged to track some fixed canon of 'the news'.

The internet is both a news medium in its own right and a connector of other media. Although the *Washington Post*'s Leonard Downie and Robert Kaiser, voices of 'old news', are snootily dismissive of the achievements of on-line journalism, and 'new news' generally, they are honest enough to note that 'in 2001, Drudge sent more readers to washingtonpost.com than did any other web site that linked to the Post.'[21] Thus does the modern news consumer rifle through both the old and the new. Tom Rosenstiel, a founder of the Committee of Concerned Journalists, and another campaigner for 'old news' values, goes further and agrees that ultimately, journalism will probably be saved by the advent of the new technologies because they create the capacity for ten young people in a garage to invent a journalism that flows out of the needs of the people they know, the communities they want to serve, rather than some sophisticated model from business consultants about how to maximise profitability. The first journalism in the 1600s was literally conversation among citizens in coffee houses in England. The internet is our new coffee house.[22]

The Age of the Virus

Advocates of public journalism are right to remind us that journalism is both a business and much more than a business. Journalism's critics do it a service by deflating its overconfidence and questioning its purpose and values. It is astonishing really that a director general of the BBC felt it necessary in 1995 to remind his colleagues in one of the biggest news organizations on earth that 'democratically elected politicians have a higher claim to speak for the people than journalists'.[23] If politics has a problem with public engagement, 'journalism is part of the problem and needs to make itself part of the solution. Journalism has got bigger, but it must not be too big for its boots: the public will not stand for that.'

As the writer on media issues Christopher Dornan has said:

20. The dotcom boom and bust came and went so fast that those reporting the story could barely keep up. This cover of a British internet magazine is dated August 2000. By February 2001, the cover of the American magazine *Fast Company* indicates the extent to which the mood had changed.

Who could have imagined that the media would come to usurp political authority, buffering the policy process and decision-makers in the chaotic turbulence of perception? In the United States of America, the most advanced and sophisticated nation on the planet, what matters now is not so much what is done, but how actions play out in the mediascape. Journalism was supposed to provide reliable records of the real. Now, it seems, a stew of journalism, entertainment and infotainment establishes what is taken to be real—not as the Chomsykites insist, according to some master plan for the manipulation of the masses, but in absurd, directionless and irrational gyrations. What Huxley and Orwell feared was the dominance of collective order over the individual. What we have arrived at is something close to the end of governance as it was once defined. When the media run the show, then the jabber and the images of the airwaves take precedence over what the images were originally meant to depict, no one is in charge.[24]

In Orwell's Room 101, Dornan points out, the authoritarian tormentor creates 'a world in which the very concept of trust has been exterminated'. But trust can be as readily lost in a mist of infotainment as in the snows of a Stalinist terror.

The first job of journalism is to find out, communicate accurately, and be trusted. If it cannot be trusted, then it will be neither believed nor respected in the judgements it makes of others. To a large extent, market mechanisms operating within a framework of strong competition policy will do the job of sorting out the trustworthy from the unreliable, but well-functioning markets also need honest, accountable suppliers, ready to correct mistakes and willing to submit to public scrutiny and debate. There is a role here for intelligent regulation and journalists would be wise to welcome it. As Onora O'Neill said in her attack upon contemporary journalism, if the news media are to be part of the solution, not part of the problem for democracy, they must provide 'reporting we can assess and check',[25] which means that free news media must collaborate with effective regulatory mechanisms to illuminate their conflicts of interest, their errors, and above all their inaccuracies. Well-run markets can deliver plurality and diversity of news provision, but trust requires something more from everyone involved in public communication: politicians, campaigners, and businesses, as well as journalists. If the politicians and business people are lying, the journalists will be thanked for saying so. If the journalists are lying, or failing to find out, there is no possibility that the public sphere will be in good health.

The danger is that the time-constrained citizen finds the whole debate encompassed in these pages too wearisome and too remote. Then, they will note the unreliability of much news and switch off, settling for a quiet life, away from the information storm. This is the great peril, the way free societies might indeed perish; lost in media space, with no direction home. Democracy needed journalism to get started. Journalism needs to re-absorb the values of democracy into its own self-conduct if it is to function effectively: to open itself to scrutiny and challenge.

There is a Chinese proverb about the dangers of failed leadership: that the fish rots from the head. In complex modern democracies, this is not so. The rot runs through a network: we are living in the age of the virus. In that sense, modern democracies are less vulnerable and more stable than those which appear to be in the grip of elites. On the other hand, once a virus gets moving, pretty soon it is everywhere and the problem cannot be solved by a change in leadership. Against such viruses, reliable, accurate, truthful journalism is the only known antidote. If the market can't deliver it, we must continue to ensure that the market failure is corrected.

By the way, when Doug Harbrecht asked Matt Drudge to name *his* greatest mistake, he replied: 'ever doubting my ability'.

Notes

Introduction

1. Macaulay wrote in the *Edinburgh Review* (Sept. 1828) that 'the (Parliamentary) gallery in which the reporters sit has become a fourth estate of the realm'. Edmund Burke had used the term earlier in the House of Commons in 1774: 'there sits a Fourth Estate more important far than they all.'
2. See www.mori.co.uk for the latest MORI opinion survey data.
3. Carl Jensen, 'What Free Press?', in Peter Philips (ed.), *Censored 2000: The Year's Top Twenty-Five Censored Stories* (New York: Seven Stories Press, 2000).
4. Ibid.
5. Bill Kovach and Tom Rosenstiel, *The Elements of Journalism: What Newspeople should Know and the Public should Expect* (New York: Crown Publishing, 2001), 13, 18, 33.
6. Vaclav Havel, 'The March of Freedom', *Press Gazette* (London 3 May 2002).
7. Onora O'Neill, *A Question of Trust.* BBC Reith Lectures, April/May 2002. www.bbc.co.uk/radio4
8. Alan Clark, in Stephen Glover (ed.), *Secrets of the Press.* (London: Penguin, 1999).
9. Janet Malcolm, *The Journalist and the Murderer* (New York: Alfred A. Knopf, 1990).
10. Leonard Downie, and Robert Kaiser, *The News about the News: American Journalism in Peril* (New York: Alfred A. Knopf, 2002).
11. Michael Bromley, 'The End of Journalism? Changes in Workplace Practices in the Press and Broadcasting In the 1990s', in M. Bromley and T. O'Malley (ed.), *A Journalism Reader.* (London: Routledge, 1997).
12. Paul Foot, 'The Slow Death of Investigative Journalism', in S. Glover (ed.), *Secrets of the Press* (London: Penguin, 1999).

13. John Pilger, *Hidden Agendas* (London: Vintage, 1998). See esp. sections 7 and 8: 'The Rise and Fall of Popular Journalism' and 'The Media Age'.

14. J. Lloyd, 'Media Manifesto', *Prospect Magazine* (London, Oct. 2002).

15. Nicholas Tomalin, 'Stop the Press, I Want to Get on', *Sunday Times* (26 Oct. 1969); reprinted in M. Bromley and T. O'Malley, *A Journalism Reader* (London: Routledge, 1997).

16. Andrew Kohut, 'Young People are Reading—Everything But Newspapers', *Columbia Journalism Review* (April 2002).

17. Ian Hargreaves and James Thomas, *New News, Old News* (London: Independent Television Commission, 2002).

18. Mitchell Stephens, *A History of News* (London: Penguin, 1988), 283.

19. Hargreaves and Thomas, *New News*, and annual reports from the Independent Television Commission's *The Public's View.*

20. John Hartley, *Popular Reality: Journalism, Modernity, Popular Culture* (London: Arnold, 1996), 32.

21. 'Internet Sapping Broadcast News'. Washington, DC: Pew Research Centre for the People and the Press, June 2000.

22. Hargreaves and Thomas, *New News.*

23. Kohut, 'Young People are Reading'.

24. Toby Mundy, *Good Books* (London: Prospect, Oct. 2002).

25. John Keane, *The Media and Democracy* (London: Polity Press, 1991).

26. W. H. Auden, 'In Memory of W. B. Yeats', *Collected Poems*, (London: Faber & Faber, 1976).

1. Born Free

1. Terror Coverage Boost News Media's Images but Military Censorship Backed, Washington DC: Pew Research Centre for the People and the Press, Nov. 2001.

2. Index on Censorships: 1 (2002).

3. John Keane, *Tom Paine, a Political Life* (London: Bloomsbury, 1995), 67.

4. Cited Hannah Barker, p 1; Newspapers, Politics and English Society: 1695–1855 (London: Longman, 1999).

5. Keane, *Tom Paine*. The quote is from John Adams.

6. Hartley, *Popular Reality*, 84.

7. Jack Richard Censer, *Prelude to Power: The Parisian Radical Press, 1789–1791* (Baltimore and London: Johns Hopkins University Press, 1976), cited in Hartley, *Popular Reality*.

8. James Mill, *Edinburgh Review* (May 1811). Reproduced in M. Bromley and T. O'Malley, *A Journalism Reader* (London: Routledge, 1997).

9. John Stuart Mill, *On Liberty*, in *Utilitarianism*, ed. H. B. Acton (London: Everyman, 1972).

10. Kevin Williams, *Get me a murder a day! A history of mass communication in Britain* (London: Arnold, 1998).

11. Ibid. 23, citing Francis Williams, *Dangerous Estate* (London: Readers Union, 1958).

12. James Curran and Jean Seaton, *Power without Responsibility: The Press and Broadcasting in Britain* (London: Routledge, 1997).

13. Williams, op cit. p. 44.

14. Ibid. 51.

15. W. T. Stead, 'The Future of Journalism', *Contemporary Review* (Nov. 1886). Reproduced in M. Bromley and T. O'Malley, *Journalism, a Reader* (London: Routledge, 1997).

16. See e.g. Mark Dery, *Escape Velocity: Cyberculture at the End of the Century*, (New York: Grove Press, 1996).

17. Roger Fidler, *Mediamorphosis: Understanding New Media*. (Thousand Oaks, Calif.: Pine Forge Press, 1997).

18. For example, an assessment of Singapore's situation by a Malaysian writer, Kokkeong Wong, proposes a 'theory of controlled commodification' to explain and justify the Singapore government's action in, on the one hand, encouraging heavy involvement of global business in Singapore's economy, while continuing to restrict global media, where they violate local political and cultural sensitivities. Kokkeong Wong, *Media and Culture in Singapore*, (Reskill, NJ; Hampton Press, 2001).

19. William De Lange, *A History of Japanese Journalism: Japan's Press Club as the*

Last Obstacle to a Mature Press. (Richmond, Surrey: Japan Library, Curzon Press, 1998), 181.

20. Adam Michnik, 'After Communism, Journalism: Ten Commandments for a Decent Journalist', *Media Studies Journal* (spring/summer 1998, Freedom Forum, New York).

21. Anthony Collings, *Words of Fire* (New York: NYU Press, 2001).

2. Big Brother

1. R. Murdoch, MacTaggart Lecture, Edinburgh Television Festival, 25 Aug. 1989.
2. Murdoch, Banqueting House speech, London, 1 Sept. 1993.
3. See Chrystia Freeland, *Sale of the Century: The Inside Story of the Second Russian Revolution* (London: Little Brown, 2000).
4. Collings, *Words of Fire*, 219.
5. *Daily Telegraph*, London, 17 Feb., 2001.
6. Frank Ellis, *From Glasnost to the Internet: Russia's New Infosphere* (London: Macmillan, 1999), 177.
7. Knowlton Nash, *Trivia Pursuit: How Showbiz Values are Corrupting the News* (Toronto: McClelland & Stewart, 1998).
8. Arthur E. Rowse, *Drive-by Journalism: The Assault on your Need to Know* (Monroe, Me: Common Courage Press, 2000).
9. Bill Kovach and Tom Rosenstiel *The Elements of Journalism: What Newspeople should Know and the Public should Expect* (New York: Crown Publishing, 2001).
10. Ibid. 33.
11. Leonard Downie and Robert Kaiser, *The News about the News: American Journalism in Peril* (New York: Alfred A. Knopf, 2002).
12. Ibid. 128.
13. For a discussion of UK data on this subject see Hargreaves and Thomas, *New News*, and regular reports from the Pew Centre.
14. Ibid., found an overwhelming majority favoured retaining current laws on impartiality and accuracy, but this support was lower in homes with multi-channel television and among younger people.

15. News International plc, Jan. 2002: 'Response to Consultation on Media Ownership Rules'. Available on www.culture.gov.uk

16. E. Lauf, 'The Vanishing Young Reader: Social-Determinants of Newspaper Use as a Source of Political Information in Europe: 1990–98', *European Journal of Communication* (2001).

17. Sian Kevill, *Beyond the Soundbite: BBC Research into Public Disillusion with Politics* (London: BBC, 2002), cited and discussed in Hargreaves and Thomas, *New News.*

18. Ibid.

19. Pierre Bourdieu, *On Television and Journalism* (Paris: Liber, 1996; English tr. London: Pluto Press, 1998).

20. Serge Halimi, *Les Nouveaux Chiens de garde* (Paris: *Liber-raisons d'agir*, 1997).

21. John Pilger, *Hidden Agendas* (London: Vintage, 1998).

22. Id., 'Freedom of the Press', *New Statesman* (London, 15 July 2002).

23. Id., *Hidden Agendas.*

24. P. Knightley, *The First Casualty: The War Correspondent as Hero and Myth-Maker from the Crimea to Kosovo* (London: Prion, 2001 edn.).

25. Ibid. 87, 88. See e.g. Susan Carruthers, *The Media at War* (London: Macmillan, 2000).

26. I. Hargreaves, 'Is there a Future for Foreign News?', *Historical Journal of Film, Radio and Television*, 20 1 (2000).

27. Bronwen Maddox, address to Centre for Journalism Studies, Cardiff University, 2002.

28. Nash, *Trivia Pursuit*, 39.

29. Hargreaves, 'Future for foreign news?'

30. Ibid.

31. Chris Cramer, 'Asleep at the Wheel', *Le Monde* (Paris, 18 Sept. 2001).

32. Brian Whitaker and Ahdaf Soueif, 'Who Needs CNN?', *Guardian* (London, 9 Oct. 2001).

33. Ibid.

34. Mohammed El-Nawawy and Adel Iskandar, *Al-Jazeera: How the Free Arab News Network Scooped the World and Changed the Middle East* (Cambridge, Mass.: Westview Press, 2002).

35. Ibid. 75.

36. Ibid. 203.

37. Carruthers, *Media at War.*

3. Star-Struck

1. 'Year Zero', *Guardian* (London, 15 July 2002).

2. Neil Postman, *Amusing Ourselves to Death* (London: Methuen 1996; 1st publ. 1985).

3. Ibid. 89–90.

4. See, e.g., Ivo Mosell (ed.), *Dumbing Down: Culture, Politics and the Mass Media (London: Imprint Academic, 2000).*

5. Matthew Engel, *Tickle the Public: 100 Years of the Popular Press* (London: Victor Gollancz, 1996), 45.

6. Bill Sloan, *I Watched a Wild Hog Eat my Baby! A Colourful History of Tabloids and their Cultural Impact* (New York: Prometheus, 2001), 15.

7. Ibid. See esp. ch. 7: 'Jackie O and the Dawn of celebrityitis'.

8. Reported in the *Guardian* (15 April 2002), media section, p. 3.

9. Nash, *Trivia Pursuit*, 189.

10. Lippman (ed.), *The Washington Post Desk-Book on Style* (New York: McGraw-Hill, 2nd edn., 1989).

11. *New York Times* (19 Nov. 2001).

12. *Wall Street Journal* (12 Oct. 2001).

13. Lecture at Cardiff University, 2001. Accessible via www.cardiff.ac.uk/jomec

14. Neal Gabler, 'The 60 Minutes Man', *Brill's Content* (May 2001).

15. In R. Snoddy, *The Good, the Bad and the Unacceptable: The Hard News about the British Press* (London: Faber & Faber, 1992).

16. K. Glynn, 'Cultural Struggle, the New News and the Politics of Popularity in the Age of Jesse "the Body" Ventura', in *Tabloid Culture* (Durham, NC: Duke University Press, 2000), 225–45.
17. Ibid.
18. Lumby, Catharine. *Gotcha: life in a tabloid world* (Sydney, Allen & Unwin. 1999), 203, 247.
19. The book maker. *Guardian*, London, 4 January, 2000.
20. David Kamp. The Tabloid Decade. *Vanity Fair*, New York, February 1999.
21. These are the central themes explored in Hargreaves and Thomas, *New News*.

4. Up to a Point, Lord Copper's

1. *The Hearsts, Father and Son* W. R. Hearst, jr., with Jack Casserly, Roberts Rinehart, Lanham, Maryland 1991.
2. Ibid.
3. W. Churchill, *The World Crisis* (1927), cited in J. Lee Thompson, *Northcliffe, Press Baron in Politics* (London: John Murray, 2000), p. xii.
4. Ibid. 209.
5. Rosenstiel and Kovach, *Elements of Journalism*, 50.
6. L. Downie and R. Kaiser, *The News about the News* (New York: Knopf, 2002), ch. 4, citing figures from Newspaper Association of America: www.naa.org/marketscope/databank
7. Bill Hagerty, *British Journalism Review*, 10 4 (2000).
8. R. Murdoch, Speech at the Banqueting House, London, 1 Sept. 1993.
9. Interview with the author, Mar. 2002. Included in BBC Radio 4 documentary, *Analysis: Free Speech for Sale*, Mar. 2002.
10. Colin Seymour-Ure, *The British Press and Broadcasting since 1945* (London: Blackwell, 1996), 49, 50.
11. Benjamin Compaine, and Douglas Gomery, *Who Owns the Media: Competition and Concentration in the Mass Media Industry*. (Mahwah, NJ: Lawrence Erlbaum, 2000), 486.

12. Ibid. 562.

13. Ibid. 505.

14. Ibid. 520, 527.

15. BBC estimates, reported in Hargreaves and Thomas, *New News.*

16. Pamela Kruger, 'The Best Way to Keep the Devil at the Door is to be Rich', *Fast Company* (New York, Nov. 2000).

17. Interview with the author, March 2002. Published *Financial Times* (2 April 2002).

18. Andrew Cameron, *Express Newspapers: The Inside Story of a Turbulent Decade.* (London: London House, 2000), 212, 213.

19. Seymour-Ure, British Press, 137.

5. Hacks v. Flaks

1. www.the451.com

2. Tom Wolfe, *Radical Chic and Mau-mauing the Flak Catchers* (New York: Farrar, Straus & Giroux, 1970).

3. Precise numbers are not available. According to David Michie's book, *The Invisible Persuaders: How Britain's Spin Doctors Manipulate the Media* (London: Bantam, 1998) Britain had 50,000 journalists and 25,000 public relations officers in the late 1990s, but the latter number was certainly growing more rapidly than the former. Michie puts the number of PR practitioners in the US at 150,000, a figure supported by Scott M. Cutlip in his history of public relations *The Unseen Power* (Hillsdale, NJ: Lawrence Erlbaum, 1994). Michie puts the number of 'reporters' in the US at 120,000.

4. Cutlip, *Unseen Power.*

5. Howard Kurtz, *The Fortune Tellers: Inside Wall Street's Game of Money, Media and Manipulation* (New York: Touchstone, 2001).

6. This brief historical account is taken largely from Cutlip, Unseen Power.

7. Ibid. 153.

8. Ibid. 178.

9. Ibid. 177.

10. Ibid. 515.
11. Ibid. 88.
12. Ibid. 602.
13. Philip Gould, *The Unfinished Revolution: How the Modernisers Saved the Labour Party* (London: Little, Brown, 1998). Refs to Abacus edn, 1999, p. 169.
14. Ibid. 334.
15. M. McLuhan, *Essential McLuhan*, ed. Eric McLuhan and Frank Zingrone. (London: Routledge, 1997), 272.
16. Piers Morgan, 'As Hugh Cudlipp said', *British Journalism Review*, 13 2, (2002).
17. Richard Lambert, 'Enron and Press'. *Prospect Magazine* (London, Mar. 2002).
18. David Kynaston, *The Financial Times A Centenary History* (London: Viking, 1998).

6. Murders is my Meat

1. Larry Langman, *The Media in the Movies: A Catalogue of American Journalism Films, 1900–1996* The precise number of films catalogued in that period is 1,025 (Jefferson, NC: McFarland, 1998).
2. Torchy Blane in *Chinatown* (1939).
3. Engel, *Tickle the Public.*
4. David Randall, *The Universal Journalist*, 2nd edn. (London: Pluto Press, 2000), 13.
5. Thomas Lippman (ed.), *The Washington Post Desk-Book on Style* (McGraw-Hill, 2nd edn., 1989).
6. Bob Steele, *Codes of Ethics and Beyond* (New York: Poynter Institute, Fla, 1999).
7. Press Complaints Commission, Editor's Code of Practice can be inspected at www.pcc.org.uk
8. Richard Shannon, *A Press Free and Responsible* (London: John Murray, 2001), 345.
9. Anna Ford, 'Only the Royals and the Very Rich are Protected from the Press', *Independent* (London, 1 Mar. 2001).

10. Shannon, *A Press Free and Responsible*, 347.
11. 'Self-censorship: How Often and Why' (Washington, DC: Pew Research Center for the People and the Press, Apr. 2000).
12. 'Striking the Balance: Audience Interests, Business Pressures and Journalists' Values' (Washington, DC: Pew Center for the People and the Press, Mar. 1999).
13. Ibid.
14. Kovach, Bill, and Rosenstiel, op cit., p. 123
15. Ibid. 20.
16. Ibid. 19.
17. Ibid. 12.
18. Jon Katz, 'Rock Rap and Music Bring you the News', *Rolling Stone* (5 Mar. 1992).
19. Anthony Browne, 'You can't Trust those Dirty, Lying Hacks', *New Statesman* (London, 10 June 2002).
20. 'Why we are Here', *British Journalism Review* (1989), Reproduced in M. Bromley T. O'Malley (eds.), *A Journalism Reader.*
21. Jeffries, Stuart. How the French lost their cleavage. *The Guardian*, London, 15 April, 2002.
22. Lippman, *Washington Post Desk-Book*, 3, 4.
23. *Journalists at Work: Journalism Training Forum* (London: Publishing NTO/Skillset, 2002); www.publishingnto.co.uk
24. American Society of Newspaper Editors, 2002 census. www.asne.org
25. David Weaver (ed.), *The Global Journalist: News People Around the World.* IAMCR (Creskill, NJ: Hampton Press, 1998).
26. John Henningham and Anthony Delano, ibid. 151.
27. Campaign 2000: Highly Rated. *Pew Center for the People and the Press* (Washington, DC, 2000).

7. Matt's Modem

1. Rupert Murdoch interview with James Harding, *Financial Times* (11 June 2002).

2. Hargreaves and Thomas, UK data suggest that only 13 per cent of people regard magazines as a useful source of news, but the same survey also shows that magazines are valued across the whole social, demographic, and ethnic spectrum.

3. Matt Drudge with Julia Phillips, *Drudge Manifesto* (New York: New American Library, 2000).

4. Matt Drudge, 'Anyone with a Modem Can Report to the World', cited in Compaine and Gomery, *Who Owns the Media.*

5. Drudge and Phillips, *Drudge Manifesto.*

6. Kovach and Rosenstiel, *Elements of Journalism.*

7. Letter to Walter James, 1813.

8. *Comparative Review of Content Regulation*, Mckinsey report for Independent Television Commission, May 2002.

9. Brian Winston, *Media Technology and Society: A History, from the Telegraph to the Internet* (London: Routledge, 1998).

10. For further discussion of this see: *When Nerds and Words Collide: reflections on the development of computer assisted reporting* (St. Petersburg, Fla: Poynter Institute, 1999).

11. The Centre for Digital Storytelling is at www.storycenter.org

12. Dana Atchley's work can be seen on his website: nextexit.com. The quote is from Greil Marcus's Invisible Republic, and features on the email tag-line of Britain's leading digital storyteller, Daniel Meadows: www.photobus.co.uk

13. Andrew Sullivan, 'Out of the Ashes, a New Way of Communicating', *Sunday Times* (London, 24 Feb. 2002); or www.andrewsullivan.com

14. For some data and discussion on the growing gaps in local news services, see Hargreaves and Thomas, *New News.*

15. 'Why I Want to Die: Revealed in her Own Words, the Agony of Woman Trapped in a Paralysed Prison', *Daily Mail* (London, 8 Mar. 2002).

16. www.indymedia.org

17. Manuel Castells, *The Internet Galaxy* (Oxford: OUP, 2001). Of the Castells trilogy, the most relevant is: *The Rise of the Network Society* (Oxford: Blackwell, 1996/2000).
18. Cassells, *Internet Galaxy*, 5.
19. Ibid. 6.
20. Ibid.
21. Leonard Downie and Robert Kaiser, *The News about the News: American Journalism in Peril* (New York: Alfred A. Knopf, 2002).
22. Interview with the author, 2001.
23. John Birt, 'For Good or Ill: The Role of the Modern Media', Independent Newspapers Annual Lecture, Dublin, Feb. 1995.
24. Christopher Dornan, 'Peering Forward', in Robert Giles, and Robert Snyder (eds.), *What's Next? Problems and Prospects of Journalism* (New Brunswick and London: Transaction, 2001).
25. Onora O'Neill, 'A Question of Trust', BBC Reith Lectures, 2002; www.bbc.co.uk/radio4

Index

Alphabetical order is word by word: a space or hyphen precedes any letter ('*New York Times*' precedes 'News Corporation'). Terms classify features of journalism, news, and truth, the principal topics of the book. An 'i' after a page number indicates inclusion of an illustration; an 'n' after a page number indicates an end-note number.

Index

Index

Index

Index

Index

Index

Index